VANNA'S
FAVORITE GIFT AFGHANS

When I was a little girl growing up in North Myrtle Beach, South Carolina, my Nana taught me my very first crochet stitches and gave me a precious gift — one that not only brings me hours of pleasure, but one that I now adore sharing with everyone I love! Handmade gifts are the best presents, especially for the person who has "everything." I get so much joy from making afghans, pillows, and dolls for my friends and family; and now I'm delighted to share my favorite gift designs with you.

Crocheted gifts are perfect for any occasion, be it a birthday, a holiday, or simply an opportunity to celebrate a friendship. Afghans make lasting mementos for milestones like weddings and births. I especially like to crochet baby blankets because they're quick to make and so fulfilling, too! In this book, you'll find afghans to suit anyone, from football fans and spirited teens to cat lovers and flower fanciers. You can even make your afghan extra-special by including a coordinating gift like a matching pillow, guardian angel, or teddy bear. They'll love it!

With the great designs and easy-to-follow instructions on these pages, I know you'll soon find your own favorites to make again and again. And I'm sure you'll agree that crocheting is not only relaxing, it's also very rewarding. After all, every stitch carries a little bit of your love to the person who receives your gift of comfort and warmth.

Vanna

EDITORIAL STAFF

Vice President and Editor-in-Chief: Anne Van Wagner Childs
Executive Director: Sandra Graham Case
Editorial Director: Susan Frantz Wiles
Publications Director: Carla Bentley
Creative Art Director: Gloria Bearden
Senior Graphics Art Director: Melinda Stout

PRODUCTION
Managing Editor: Susan White Sullivan
Senior Technical Editor: Cathy Hardy
Instructional Editor: Tammy Kreimeyer

EDITORIAL
Managing Editor: Linda L. Trimble
Associate Editor: Terri Leming Davidson
Assistant Editors: Janice Teipen Wojcik and
    Stacey Robertson Marshall

ART
Book/Magazine Graphics Art Director: Diane Thomas
Senior Graphics Illustrator: Linda Chambers

PROMOTIONS
Managing Editors: Alan Caudle
Associate Editor: Steven M. Cooper
Designer: Dale Rowett
Art Director: Linda Lovette Smart
Publishing Systems Administrator: Cynthia M. Lumpkin
Publishing Systems Assistant: Susan Mary Gray

BUSINESS STAFF

Publisher: Rick Barton
Vice President and General Manager: Thomas L. Carlisle
Vice President, Finance: Tom Siebenmorgen
Vice President, Retail Marketing: Bob Humphrey
Vice President, National Accounts: Pam Stebbins
Retail Marketing Director: Margaret Sweetin
General Merchandise Manager: Cathy Laird
Vice President, Operations: Brian U. Davis
Distribution Director: Rob Thieme
Retail Customer Service Director: Tonie B. Maulding
Retail Customer Service Managers: Carolyn Pruss and Wanda Price
Print Production Manager: Fred F. Pruss

Vanna's Favorite Gift Afghans
from the Crochet Treasury Series
Published by Leisure Arts, Inc., and Oxmoor House, Inc.

Library of Congress Catalog Number 98-66055
Hardcover ISBN 1-57486-134-4
Softcover ISBN 1-57486-135-2

2

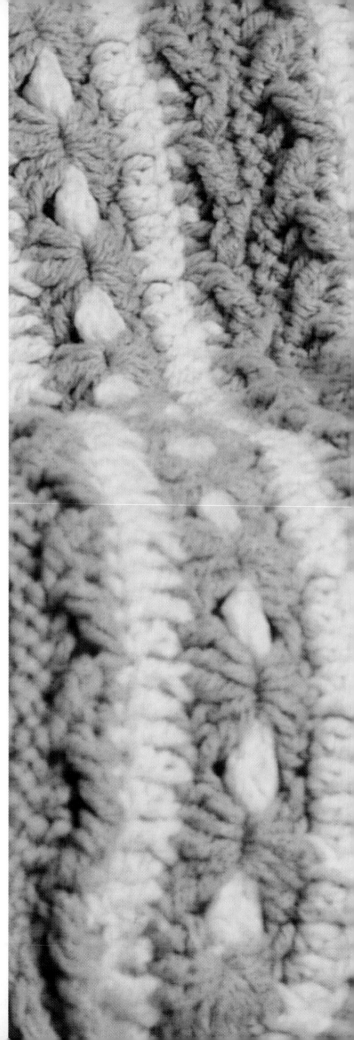

TABLE OF CONTENTS

HAPPY ANNIVERSARY

Present an enduring gift of love to help a favorite couple celebrate their years of wedded bliss. The interlaced links symbolize the joyous life they've built together.

INTERLACED LINKS

Finished Size: 47" x 61"

MATERIALS
Worsted Weight Yarn:
  Green - 46 ounces, (1,310 grams, 3,025 yards)
  Off-White - 33 ounces, (940 grams, 2,170 yards)
Crochet hook, size K (6.50 mm) **or** size needed
  for gauge
Yarn needle

Note: Afghan is worked holding two strands of yarn
  together throughout.

GAUGE: Each Strip = 5³⁄₄" wide

Gauge Swatch: 3¹⁄₂" in diameter
Work same as First Ring.

STITCH GUIDE

REVERSE SINGLE CROCHET
  (abbreviated reverse sc)
Working from **left** to **right**, insert hook in sc to right of
hook, YO and draw through, under, and to left of loop
on hook (2 loops on hook), YO and draw through both
loops on hook *(Figs. 19a-d, page 125)*.

PUFF STITCH *(abbreviated Puff St)*
★ YO, insert hook in sc indicated, YO and pull up a loop
even with loop on hook; repeat from ★ 2 times **more**,
YO and draw through all 7 loops on hook *(Fig. 1)*.

Fig. 1

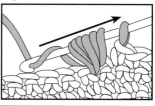

STRIP (Make 8)
CENTER
FIRST RING
With Green, ch 16; join with slip st to form a ring.
Rnd 1 (Right side)**:** Ch 1, 28 sc in ring; join with slip st to
first sc.
Note: Loop a short piece of yarn around any stitch to mark
Rnd 1 as **right** side and bottom edge.
Rnd 2: Ch 3, skip next sc, (slip st in next sc, ch 3, skip
next sc) around; join with slip st to first slip st, finish off:
14 ch-3 sps.

SECOND RING
With Off-White, ch 16; with **right** side of previous ring
facing, insert end of ch from **front** to **back** through center
of last ring made; join with slip st to form a ring.
Rnd 1 (Right side)**:** Ch 1, 28 sc in ring; join with slip st to
first sc.
Note: Mark Rnd 1 as **right** side.
Rnd 2: Ch 3, skip next sc, (slip st in next sc, ch 3, skip
next sc) around; join with slip st to first slip st, finish off:
14 ch-3 sps.

THIRD RING
With Green, ch 16; with **right** side of previous ring facing,
insert end of ch from **front** to **back** through center of last
ring made; join with slip st to form a ring.
Rnd 1 (Right side)**:** Ch 1, 28 sc in ring; join with slip st to
first sc.
Note: Mark Rnd 1 as **right** side.
Rnd 2: Ch 3, skip next sc, (slip st in next sc, ch 3, skip
next sc) around; join with slip st to first slip st, finish off:
14 ch-3 sps.

REMAINING 24 RINGS
Repeat Second and Third Rings, 12 times: 27 Rings.

Instructions continued on page 100.

VALENTINE'S DAY

Romance your sweetheart with this Victorian-style throw that's laced with airy hearts. It's a lovely way to "whisper" sweet nothings to your valentine!

LOVING HEARTS

Finished Size: 46" x 64"

MATERIALS
Worsted Weight Yarn:
34 ounces, (970 grams, 1,920 yards)
Crochet hook, size I (5.50 mm) **or** size needed for gauge

GAUGE: Each Motif = 6" square

Gauge Swatch: 2" square
Work same as Motif through Rnd 1.

STITCH GUIDE

2-DC CLUSTER
★ YO, insert hook in st or sp indicated, YO and pull up a loop, YO and draw through 2 loops on hook; repeat from ★ once **more**, YO and draw through all 3 loops on hook *(Figs. 16a & b, page 124)*.

3-DC CLUSTER
★ YO, insert hook in st or sp indicated, YO and pull up a loop, YO and draw through 2 loops on hook; repeat from ★ 2 times **more**, YO and draw through all 4 loops on hook.

DECREASE
Pull up a loop in next 2 sc, YO and draw through all 3 loops on hook.

FIRST MOTIF
Ch 4; join with slip st to form a ring.
Rnd 1 (Right side): Ch 2, work 2-dc Cluster in ring, ch 4, (work 3-dc Cluster in ring, ch 4) 4 times; join with slip st to top of first Cluster: 5 ch-4 sps.
Note: Loop a short piece of yarn around any stitch to mark Rnd 1 as **right** side.
Rnd 2: Slip st in first ch-4 sp, ch 1, (sc, ch 3, sc) in same sp, ★ (ch 3, sc) 3 times in next ch-4 sp, (ch 3, sc) twice in next ch-4 sp; repeat from ★ once **more**, ch 1, hdc in first sc to form last sp: 12 sps.
Rnd 3: Ch 1, sc in same sp, ch 3, sc in next ch-3 sp, ch 3, (work 3-dc Cluster, ch 3) twice in next ch-3 sp, ★ (sc in next ch-3 sp, ch 3) twice, (work 3-dc Cluster, ch 3) twice in next ch-3 sp; repeat from ★ around; join with slip st to first sc: 8 Clusters and 16 ch-3 sps.
Rnd 4: Slip st in first ch-3 sp, ch 8, dc in same sp, ch 5, skip next ch-3 sp, work (3-dc Cluster, ch 3, 3-dc Cluster) in next corner ch-3 sp, ch 5, skip next ch-3 sp, ★ (dc, ch 5) twice in next ch-3 sp, skip next ch-3 sp, work (3-dc Cluster, ch 3, 3-dc Cluster) in next corner ch-3 sp, ch 5, skip next ch-3 sp; repeat from ★ around; join with slip st to third ch of beginning ch-8.
Rnd 5: Slip st in first ch-5 sp, ch 1, sc in same sp, ch 5, sc in next ch-5 sp, ch 5, (sc, ch 7, sc) in next corner ch-3 sp, ch 5, ★ (sc in next ch-5 sp, ch 5) 3 times, (sc, ch 7, sc) in next corner ch-3 sp, ch 5; repeat from ★ around to last ch-5 sp, sc in last ch-5 sp, ch 5; join with slip st to first sc, finish off.

REMAINING MOTIFS
Work same as First Motif through Rnd 4.
Work One Side or Two Side Joining to form 6 vertical strips of 9 Motifs each.
Note: When working into corner loop that has been previously joined, work into joining sc.

ONE SIDE JOINING
Rnd 5 (Joining rnd): Slip st in first ch-5 sp, ch 1, sc in same sp, ch 5, sc in next ch-5 sp, ch 5, ★ (sc, ch 7, sc) in next corner ch-3 sp, ch 5, (sc in next ch-5 sp, ch 5) 3 times; repeat from ★ once **more**, sc in next corner ch-3 sp, ch 3, with **wrong** sides together, sc in corresponding corner ch-7 sp on **previous** Motif *(Fig. 24, page 126)*, ch 3, sc in same sp on **new** Motif, ch 2, sc in next ch-5 sp on **previous** Motif, ch 2, (sc in next ch-5 sp on **new** Motif, ch 2, sc in next ch-5 sp on **previous** Motif, ch 2) 3 times, sc in next corner ch-3 sp on **new** Motif, ch 3, sc in next corner ch-7 sp on **previous** Motif, ch 3, sc in same sp on **new** Motif, ch 5, sc in next ch-5 sp, ch 5; join with slip st to first sc, finish off.

Instructions continued on page 100.

*"When I give to you
what I make with my hands,
I share my heart."*

WELCOME, NEIGHBOR!

A new neighbor will feel right at home when you give this welcoming wrap. The lacy pineapples, symbols of hospitality, extend a warm greeting to your new friend.

WELCOME PINEAPPLES

Finished Size: 42½" x 62½"

MATERIALS
Worsted Weight Yarn:
  37 ounces, (1,050 grams, 2,535 yards)
Crochet hook, size H (5.00 mm) **or** size needed for gauge
Yarn needle

GAUGE: 13 dc = 4"; 8 rows = 4¼"
  Each Panel = 10½"w

Gauge Swatch: 4"w x 4¼"h
Ch 15 **loosely**.
Row 1: Dc in fourth ch from hook **(3 skipped chs counts as first dc)** and in each ch across: 13 dc.
Rows 2-8: Ch 3 **(counts as first dc)**, turn; dc in next dc and in each dc across.
Finish off.

STITCH GUIDE

REVERSE SINGLE CROCHET
(abbreviated reverse sc)
Working from **left** to **right**, insert hook in st to right of hook, YO and draw through, under, and to left of loop on hook (2 loops on hook), YO and draw through both loops on hook *(Figs. 19a-d, page 125)*.

Note: Each row is worked across length of Afghan.

PANEL (Make 4)
Ch 206 **loosely**, place marker in fourth ch from hook for st placement.
Row 1: Working in back ridges of beginning ch *(Fig. 2b, page 122)*, dc in sixth ch from hook, ★ ch 1, skip next ch, dc in next 30 chs, ch 1, skip next ch, dc in next ch; repeat from ★ across to last 2 chs, ch 1, skip next ch, dc in last ch: 188 dc and 14 sps.
Row 2: Ch 4 **(counts as first dc plus ch 1, now and throughout)**, turn; dc in next dc, ch 1, ★ dc in each dc across to next ch-1 sp, ch 1, dc in next dc, ch 1; repeat from ★ across to last sp, skip next ch, dc in next ch: 189 dc and 14 ch-1 sps.
Row 3: Ch 4, turn; dc in next dc, ch 1, ★ dc in next 13 dc, ch 1, skip next dc, dc in next dc, ch 5, dc in next dc, ch 1, skip next dc, dc in next 13 dc, ch 1, dc in next dc, ch 1; repeat from ★ across to last dc, dc in last dc: 177 dc and 32 sps.
Row 4: Ch 4, turn; dc in next dc, ch 1, ★ dc in next 10 dc, ch 3, skip next 3 dc and next ch-1 sp, 11 dc in ch-5 sp, ch 3, skip next 4 dc, dc in next 10 dc, ch 1, dc in next dc, ch 1; repeat from ★ across to last dc, dc in last dc: 195 dc and 26 sps.
Row 5: Ch 4, turn; dc in next dc, ch 1, ★ dc in next 6 dc, ch 3, skip next 4 dc, dc in next dc, (ch 1, dc in next dc) 10 times, ch 3, skip next 4 dc, dc in next 6 dc, ch 1, dc in next dc, ch 1; repeat from ★ across to last dc, dc in last dc: 147 dc and 86 sps.
Row 6: Ch 4, turn; dc in next dc, ch 1, ★ dc in next 4 dc, 2 dc in next dc, ch 3, skip next dc and next ch-3 sp, (sc in next ch-1 sp, ch 3) 10 times, skip next ch-3 sp and next dc, 2 dc in next dc, dc in next 4 dc, ch 1, dc in next dc, ch 1; repeat from ★ across to last dc, dc in last dc: 81 dc and 80 sps.
Row 7: Ch 4, turn; dc in next dc, ch 1, ★ dc in next 4 dc, 2 dc in next dc, ch 3, skip next dc and next ch-3 sp, (sc in next ch-3 sp, ch 3) 9 times, skip next ch-3 sp and next dc, 2 dc in next dc, dc in next 4 dc, ch 1, dc in next dc, ch 1; repeat from ★ across to last dc, dc in last dc: 81 dc and 74 sps.
Row 8: Ch 4, turn; dc in next dc, ch 1, ★ dc in next 4 dc, 2 dc in next dc, ch 3, skip next dc and next ch-3 sp, (sc in next ch-3 sp, ch 3) 8 times, skip next ch-3 sp and next dc, 2 dc in next dc, dc in next 4 dc, ch 1, dc in next dc, ch 1; repeat from ★ across to last dc, dc in last dc; do **not** finish off: 81 dc and 68 sps.

Instructions continued on page 101.

9

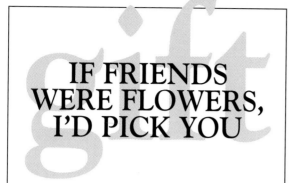

IF FRIENDS WERE FLOWERS, I'D PICK YOU

When I indulge a friend with a lavish afghan like this one, she knows just how special our friendship is to me. This lacy throw lets her sleep in a "bed of roses" every night.

BED OF ROSES

Finished Size: 48" x 67"

MATERIALS

Worsted Weight Yarn:
    Natural - 31 ounces, (880 grams, 2,125 yards)
    Rose - 13 ounces, (370 grams, 890 yards)
    Green - 6 ounces, (170 grams, 410 yards)
Crochet hook, size I (5.50 mm) **or** size needed for gauge

GAUGE: Each Square = 9½"

Gauge Swatch: 3" square
Work same as First Square through Rnd 2.

STITCH GUIDE

BEGINNING POPCORN
Ch 3, 3 dc in sp indicated, drop loop from hook, insert hook in top of beginning ch-3, hook dropped loop and draw through *(Fig. 18, page 124)*.
POPCORN
4 Dc in sp indicated, drop loop from hook, insert hook in first dc of 4-dc group, hook dropped loop and draw through.
V-ST
(Dc, ch 1, dc) in sp indicated.

FIRST SQUARE

With Rose, ch 4; join with slip st to form a ring.
Rnd 1 (Right side): Work beginning Popcorn in ring, ch 3, (work Popcorn in ring, ch 3) 3 times; join with slip st to top of beginning Popcorn: 4 ch-3 sps.
Rnd 2: Slip st in first ch-3 sp, ch 1, work (sc, dc, 2 tr, dc, sc, slip st, ch 1) twice in each ch-3 sp around; join with slip st to first sc: 8 petals.
Rnd 3: Ch 5, working **behind** petals on Rnd 2, (slip st in next ch-1 sp, ch 5) around; join with slip st to first st: 8 ch-5 sps.
Rnd 4: Slip st in first ch-5 sp, ch 1, work (sc, dc, 5 tr, dc, sc, ch 1) in same sp and in each ch-5 sp around; join with slip st to first sc: 8 petals.
Rnd 5: Ch 5, working **behind** petals on Rnd 4, (slip st in next ch-1 sp, ch 5) around; join with slip st to first st, finish off: 8 ch-5 sps.
Rnd 6: With **right** side facing, join Green with slip st in any ch-5 sp; ch 4 **(counts as first dc plus ch 1, now and throughout)**, in same sp work [dc, (ch 1, dc) twice, ch 3, (dc, ch 1) 4 times], (dc, ch 1) twice in next ch-5 sp, ★ in next ch-5 sp work [dc, (ch 1, dc) 3 times, ch 3, (dc, ch 1) 4 times], (dc, ch 1) twice in next ch-5 sp; repeat from ★ around; join with slip st to first dc, finish off: 40 dc.
Rnd 7: With **right** side facing, join Natural with slip st in any corner ch-3 sp; ch 4, (dc, ch 3, work V-St) in same sp, ch 1, ★ skip next ch-1 sp, (work V-St in next ch-1 sp, ch 1, skip next ch-1 sp) 4 times, work (V-St, ch 3, V-St) in next corner ch-3 sp, ch 1; repeat from ★ 2 times **more**, skip next ch-1 sp, (work V-St in next ch-1 sp, ch 1, skip next ch-1 sp) across; join with slip st to first dc: 24 V-Sts.
Rnd 8: Turn; slip st in first ch-1 sp, ch 4, dc in same sp, ch 1, ★ skip next V-St, (work V-St in next ch-1 sp, ch 1, skip next V-St) across to next corner ch-3 sp, work (V-St, ch 3, V-St) in corner ch-3 sp, ch 1; repeat from ★ 3 times **more**, skip last V-St; join with slip st to first dc: 28 V-Sts.
Rnd 9: Turn; slip st in first ch-1 sp, ch 4, dc in same sp, skip next V-St, work (V-St, ch 3, V-St) in next corner ch-3 sp, ★ (skip next V-St, work V-St in next ch-1 sp) 6 times, skip next V-St, work (V-St, ch 3, V-St) in next corner ch-3 sp; repeat from ★ 2 times **more**, skip next V-St, (work V-St in next ch-1 sp, skip next V-St) across; join with slip st to first dc: 32 V-Sts.
Rnd 10: Do **not** turn; slip st in first ch-1 sp, ch 3 **(counts as first dc)**, 2 dc in same sp, 3 dc in next V-St (ch-1 sp), ★ (2 dc, ch 3, 2 dc) in next corner ch-3 sp, 3 dc in each V-St across; repeat from ★ around; join with slip st to first dc; do **not** finish off: 112 dc.

Instructions continued on page 102.

BIRTHDAY JEWELS

Choose yarn in the appropriate hue to stitch up a regal birthstone wrap. The birth month guide will help you match the right jewel for your "precious" birthday boy or girl.

BIRTHSTONE WRAP

Finished Size: 47" x 61"

MATERIALS
Worsted Weight Yarn:
  85 ounces, (2,410 grams, 5,830 yards)
Crochet hook, size I (5.50 mm) **or** size needed for gauge

MONTH	BIRTHSTONE
January	Garnet
February	Amethyst
March	Aquamarine
April	Diamond
May	Emerald
June	Pearl
July	Ruby
August	Peridot
September	Sapphire
October	Opal
November	Topaz
December	Turquoise

GAUGE: In pattern, 17 sts and 10 rows = 4"

Gauge Swatch: 11"w x 4"h
Ch 48 **loosely**.
Work same as Afghan Body for 10 rows.
Finish off.

STITCH GUIDE

FRONT POST DOUBLE CROCHET
  (abbbreviated FPdc)
YO, insert hook from **front** to **back** around post of st indicated, YO and pull up a loop *(Fig. 11, page 123)*, (YO and draw through 2 loops on hook) twice. Skip st behind FPdc.

BACK POST DOUBLE CROCHET
  (abbreviated BPdc)
YO, insert hook from **back** to **front** around post of st indicated, YO and pull up a loop *(Fig. 14, page 124)*, (YO and draw through 2 loops on hook) twice. Skip st in front of BPdc.

FRONT POST TREBLE CROCHET
  (abbreviated FPtr)
YO twice, insert hook from **front** to **back** around post of st indicated, YO and pull up a loop *(Fig. 12, page 124)*, (YO and draw through 2 loops on hook) 3 times. Skip st behind FPtr.

BACK POST TREBLE CROCHET
  (abbreviated BPtr)
YO twice, insert hook from **back** to **front** around post of st indicated, YO and pull up a loop *(Fig. 15, page 124)*, (YO and draw through 2 loops on hook) 3 times. Skip st in front of BPtr.

AFGHAN BODY
Ch 198 **loosely**.
Row 1: Dc in fourth ch from hook **(3 skipped chs count as first dc)** and in each ch across: 196 dc.
Row 2 (Right side): Ch 2 **(counts as first hdc, now and throughout)**, turn; ★ † work FPdc around each of next 2 dc, (dc in next 2 dc, work FPdc around each of next 2 dc) 3 times †, work BPdc around each of next 2 dc, work FPdc around next dc, work BPdc around each of next 2 dc, skip next 3 dc, work FPtr around each of next 3 dc, working in **front** of 3 FPtr just made, work FPtr around each of 3 skipped dc, work BPdc around each of next 2 dc, work FPdc around next dc, work BPdc around each of next 2 dc; repeat from ★ across to last 15 dc, then repeat from † to † once, hdc in last dc.
Note: Loop a short piece of yarn around any stitch to mark Row 2 as **right** side.
Row 3: Ch 2, turn; ★ † dc in next 2 FPdc, (work FPdc around each of next 2 dc, dc in next 2 FPdc) 3 times †, work FPdc around each of next 2 BPdc, work BPdc around next FPdc, work FPdc around each of next 2 BPdc, work BPdc around each of next 6 FPtr, work FPdc around each of next 2 BPdc, work BPdc around next FPdc, work FPdc around each of next 2 BPdc; repeat from ★ across to last 15 sts, then repeat from † to † once, hdc in last hdc; do **not** finish off.

Instructions continued on page 102.

YOU'RE A "PURR-FECT" PAL

*Tell a friend that
she's just "purr-fect"
with this cozy coverlet!
The sweet kitty cat
silhouettes are created
with cluster stitches.*

KITTY CAT CLUSTERS

Finished Size: 53" x 72"

MATERIALS
Worsted Weight Yarn:
    Ecru - 49 ounces, (1,390 grams, 3,360 yards)
    Green - 7 ounces, (200 grams, 480 yards)
Crochet hook, size I (5.50 mm) **or** size needed for gauge
Yarn needle

GAUGE: Each Square = 9½"

Gauge Swatch: 3½" square
Ch 14 **loosely.**
Row 1 (Right side): Sc in second ch from hook, ★ ch 1,
skip next ch, sc in next ch; repeat from ★ across: 7 sc and
6 ch-1 sps.
Rows 2-13: Ch 1, turn; sc in first sc, (ch 1, sc in next sc)
across.
Finish off.

STITCH GUIDE

CLUSTER
YO, insert hook in Back Loop Only of next ch (*Fig. 20,
page 125*), YO and pull up a loop, YO and draw through
2 loops on hook, YO, insert hook in same ch, YO and
pull up a loop, YO and draw through 2 loops on hook,
YO and draw through all 3 loops on hook (*Figs. 16a & b,
page 124*). Push Cluster to right side.

SQUARE (Make 35)
With Ecru, ch 28 **loosely.**
Row 1 (Right side): Sc in second ch from hook, ★ ch 1,
skip next ch, sc in next ch; repeat from ★ across:
14 sc and 13 ch-1 sps.
Note: Loop a short piece of yarn around any stitch to mark
Row 1 as **right** side and bottom edge.
Rows 2 and 3: Ch 1, turn; sc in first sc, (ch 1, sc in
next sc) across.
Row 4: Ch 1, turn; sc in first sc, (ch 1, sc in next sc)
3 times, (work Cluster, sc in next sc) 5 times, (ch 1, sc in
next sc) across: 5 Clusters.
Row 5: Ch 1, turn; sc in first sc, (ch 1, sc in next sc)
across.
Row 6: Ch 1, turn; sc in first sc, (ch 1, sc in next sc)
twice, (work Cluster, sc in next sc) 8 times, (ch 1, sc in
next sc) across: 8 Clusters.
Row 7: Ch 1, turn; sc in first sc, (ch 1, sc in next sc)
across.
Row 8: Ch 1, turn; sc in first sc, (ch 1, sc in next sc)
twice, (work Cluster, sc in next sc) 7 times, ch 1,
sc in next sc, work Cluster, sc in next sc, (ch 1, sc in
next sc) twice: 8 Clusters.
Row 9: Ch 1, turn; sc in first sc, (ch 1, sc in next sc)
across.
Row 10: Ch 1, turn; sc in first sc, (ch 1, sc in next sc)
twice, (work Cluster, sc in next sc) 7 times, (ch 1, sc in
next sc) twice, work Cluster, sc in next sc, ch 1, sc in
last sc: 8 Clusters.
Row 11: Ch 1, turn; sc in first sc, (ch 1, sc in next sc)
across.
Rows 12 and 13: Repeat Rows 10 and 11.
Row 14: Ch 1, turn; sc in first sc, (ch 1, sc in next sc)
3 times, (work Cluster, sc in next sc) 5 times, (ch 1,
sc in next sc) 3 times, work Cluster, sc in next sc, ch 1,
sc in last sc: 6 Clusters.
Row 15: Ch 1, turn; sc in first sc, (ch 1, sc in next sc)
across.
Row 16: Ch 1, turn; sc in first sc, (ch 1, sc in next sc)
4 times, (work Cluster, sc in next sc) 3 times, (ch 1, sc in
next sc) 3 times, work Cluster, sc in next sc, (ch 1, sc in
next sc) twice: 4 Clusters.
Row 17: Ch 1, turn; sc in first sc, (ch 1, sc in next sc)
across.
Rows 18-23: Repeat Rows 4 and 5, 3 times.
Row 24: Ch 1, turn; sc in first sc, ★ (ch 1, sc in next sc)
3 times, work Cluster, sc in next sc; repeat from ★ once
more, (ch 1, sc in next sc) across: 2 Clusters.
Rows 25 and 26: Ch 1, turn; sc in first sc, (ch 1, sc in
next sc) across; do **not** finish off.

Instructions continued on page 103.

TO MY BROTHER

*I made a handsome wrap
like this one for my
younger brother, Chip.
The manly ripple pattern
is a distinctive touch
for his den.*

MOUNTAIN TRAILS

Finished Size: 48" x 71"

MATERIALS
Worsted Weight Yarn:
    Burgundy - 26 ounces, (740 grams, 1,785 yards)
    Natural - 17 ounces, (480 grams, 1,195 yards)
    Green - 2 ounces, (60 grams, 135 yards)
Crochet hooks, sizes H (5.00 mm) **and** I (5.50 mm) **or**
sizes needed for gauge

GAUGE: Each repeat from point to point = 6";
       7 rows = 4¼"

Gauge Swatch: 12"w x 4¼"h
With small size hook, ch 50 **loosely**.
Work same as Afghan for 7 rows.

STITCH GUIDE

DC DECREASE
★ YO, insert hook in **next** st or sp, YO and pull up a
loop, YO and draw through 2 loops on hook; repeat from
★ once **more**, YO and draw through all 3 loops on hook
(**counts as one dc**).

SC DECREASE
Pull up a loop in next 2 sts, YO and draw through all
3 loops on hook (**counts as one sc**).

AFGHAN

With small size hook and Burgundy, ch 206 **loosely**.
Row 1 (Right side): Dc in third ch from hook and in next
9 chs, (dc, ch 3, dc) in next ch, dc in next 9 chs, dc decrease,
★ skip next 3 chs, dc decrease, dc in next 9 chs, (dc, ch 3,
dc) in next ch, dc in next 9 chs, dc decrease; repeat from ★
across: 176 dc.
Note: Loop a short piece of yarn around any stitch to mark
Row 1 as **right** side.
Rows 2-4: Ch 2, turn; dc in next 10 dc, (dc, ch 3, dc) in
next ch-3 sp, dc in next 9 dc, ★ dc decrease twice, dc in next
9 dc, (dc, ch 3, dc) in next ch-3 sp, dc in next 9 dc; repeat
from ★ across to last 2 dc, dc decrease; at end of Row 4,
finish off.
Row 5: With **right** side facing and small size hook, join
Natural with slip st in first dc; ch 2, dc in next 10 dc,
(dc, ch 3, dc) in next ch-3 sp, dc in next 9 dc, ★ dc decrease
twice, dc in next 9 dc, (dc, ch 3, dc) in next ch-3 sp, dc in
next 9 dc; repeat from ★ across to last 2 dc, dc decrease.
Rows 6 and 7: Ch 2, turn; dc in next 10 dc, (dc, ch 3, dc)
in next ch-3 sp, dc in next 9 dc, ★ dc decrease twice,
dc in next 9 dc, (dc, ch 3, dc) in next ch-3 sp, dc in next
9 dc; repeat from ★ across to last 2 dc, dc decrease; at end
of Row 7, finish off.
Row 8: With **wrong** side facing and large size hook, join
Burgundy with slip st in first dc; ch 1, pull up a loop in same
st and in next dc, YO and draw through all 3 loops on hook,
ch 1, skip next dc, (sc in next dc, ch 1, skip next dc) 4 times,
(sc, ch 3, sc) in next ch-3 sp, ch 1, (skip next dc, sc in next
dc, ch 1) 4 times, ★ skip next dc, sc decrease twice, ch 1,
skip next dc, (sc in next dc, ch 1, skip next dc) 4 times,
(sc, ch 3, sc) in next ch-3 sp, ch 1, (skip next dc, sc in next
dc, ch 1) 4 times; repeat from ★ across to last 3 dc, skip next
dc, sc decrease; finish off: 88 sps.
Row 9: With **right** side facing and large size hook, join
Green with slip st in first sc; ch 1, pull up a loop in same st
and in next ch-1 sp, YO and draw through all 3 loops on
hook, ch 1, (sc in next ch-1 sp, ch 1) 4 times, (sc, ch 3, sc)
in next ch-3 sp, ch 1, ★ (sc in next ch-1 sp, ch 1) 10 times,
(sc, ch 3, sc) in next ch-3 sp, ch 1; repeat from ★ across to
last 5 ch-1 sps, (sc in next ch-1 sp, ch 1) 4 times, pull up a
loop in next ch-1 sp and in last st, YO and draw through all
3 loops on hook; finish off: 95 sps.
Row 10: With **wrong** side facing and large size hook, join
Burgundy with slip st in first st; ch 1, pull up a loop in same
st and in next ch-1 sp, YO and draw through all 3 loops on
hook, ch 1, (sc in next ch-1 sp, ch 1) 4 times, (sc, ch 3, sc)
in next ch-3 sp, ch 1, ★ (sc in next ch-1 sp, ch 1) 5 times,
skip next ch-1 sp, (sc in next ch-1 sp, ch 1) 5 times,
(sc, ch 3, sc) in next ch-3 sp, ch 1; repeat from ★ across
to last 5 ch-1 sps, (sc in next ch-1 sp, ch 1) 4 times, pull up
a loop in next ch-1 sp and in last st, YO and draw through
all 3 loops on hook; finish off.

Instructions continued on page 104.

16

Present this floral-motif afghan to the dear sister who's helped you through it all. It's a beautiful way to wrap her in love.

MAGNOLIA

Finished Size: 51" x 71"

MATERIALS
Worsted Weight Yarn:
Green - 36 ounces, (1,020 grams, 2,280 yards)
Off-White - 12½ ounces, (360 grams, 790 yards)
Crochet hook, size I (5.50 mm) **or** size needed for gauge
Yarn needle

GAUGE: Each Square = 5"

Gauge Swatch: 2¾"
Work same as Square Rnds 1 and 2.

STITCH GUIDE

V-STITCH *(abbreviated V-St)*
(Dc, ch 1, dc) in sp indicated.

SQUARE (Make 117)
Rnd 1 (Right side): With Green, ch 4, 2 dc in fourth ch from hook, ch 3, (3 dc in same ch, ch 3) 3 times; join with slip st to top of beginning ch-4, finish off: 4 ch-3 sps.
Note: Loop a short piece of yarn around any stitch to mark Rnd 1 as **right** side.

Rnd 2: With **right** side facing, join Off-White with slip st in any ch-3 sp; ch 3 **(counts as first dc, now and throughout)**, (2 dc, ch 3, 3 dc) in same sp, ch 1, ★ (3 dc, ch 3, 3 dc) in next ch-3 sp, ch 1; repeat from ★ 2 times **more**; join with slip st to first dc, finish off: 8 sps.
Rnd 3: With **right** side facing, join Green with slip st in any corner ch-3 sp; ch 6, (dc, ch 5, dc, ch 3, dc) in same sp, (dc, ch 3, dc) in next ch-1 sp, ★ (dc, ch 3, dc, ch 5, dc, ch 3, dc) in next ch-3 sp, (dc, ch 3, dc) in next ch-1 sp; repeat from ★ 2 times **more**; join with slip st to third ch of beginning ch-6: 16 sps.
Rnd 4: Slip st in next ch and in same sp, ch 4, work (V-St, ch 3, V-St) in next ch-5 sp, ch 1, dc in next ch-3 sp, ch 1, work V-St in next ch-3 sp, ch 1, ★ dc in next ch-3 sp, ch 1, work (V-St, ch 3, V-St) in next ch-5 sp, ch 1, dc in next ch-3 sp, ch 1, work V-St in next ch-3 sp, ch 1; repeat from ★ 2 times **more**; join with slip st to third ch of beginning ch-4, finish off: 32 sps.

ASSEMBLY
With Green and working through both loops, whipstitch Squares together *(Fig. 26b, page 126)*, forming 9 vertical strips of 13 Squares each, beginning in center ch of first corner ch-3 and ending in center ch of next corner ch-3; whipstitch strips together in same manner.

EDGING
Rnd 1: With **right** side facing, join Green with sc in any corner ch-3 sp *(see Joining With Sc, page 125)*; ch 2, sc in same sp, ch 1, (sc in next sp, ch 1) across to next corner ch-3 sp, ★ (sc, ch 2, sc) in corner ch-3 sp, ch 1, (sc in next sp, ch 1) across to next corner ch-3 sp; repeat from ★ 2 times **more**; join with slip st to first sc: 396 sps.
Rnd 2: Ch 1, (sc, ch 2, sc) in first ch-2 sp, ch 1, (sc in next ch-1 sp, ch 1) across to next corner ch-2 sp, ★ (sc, ch 2, sc) in corner ch-2 sp, ch 1, (sc in next ch-1 sp, ch 1) across to next corner ch-2 sp; repeat from ★ 2 times **more**; join with slip st to first sc, finish off: 400 sps.
Rnd 3: With **right** side facing, join Off-White with slip st in any corner ch-2 sp; ch 3, (2 dc, ch 3, 3 dc) in same sp, ch 1, skip next ch-1 sp, (3 dc in next ch-1 sp, ch 1, skip next ch-1 sp) across to next corner ch-2 sp, ★ (3 dc, ch 3, 3 dc) in corner ch-2 sp, ch 1, skip next ch-1 sp, (3 dc in next ch-1 sp, ch 1, skip next ch-1 sp) across to next corner ch-2 sp; repeat from ★ 2 times **more**; join with slip st to first dc, finish off: 204 sps.
Rnd 4: With **right** side facing, join Green with slip st in any corner ch-3 sp; ch 3, (2 dc, ch 3, 3 dc) in same sp, ch 1, (3 dc in next ch-1 sp, ch 1) across to next corner ch-3 sp, ★ (3 dc, ch 3, 3 dc) in corner ch-3 sp, ch 1, (3 dc in next ch-1 sp, ch 1) across to next corner ch-3 sp; repeat from ★ 2 times **more**; join with slip st to first dc, finish off: 208 sps.

Instructions continued on page 104.

FOR AN OLD-FASHIONED FRIEND

This quilt-inspired design is a delightfully old-fashioned gift for an old-fashioned friend! Known as Attic Windows, the design provides a wistful peek into days gone by.

ATTIC WINDOWS

Finished Size: 50" x 62"

MATERIALS
Worsted Weight Yarn:
    Teal - 14 ounces, (400 grams, 920 yards)
    Lt Teal - 14 ounces, (400 grams, 920 yards)
    Tan - 13 ounces, (370 grams, 855 yards)
    Gold - 9 ounces, (260 grams, 595 yards)
    Brown - 8 ounces, (230 grams, 525 yards)
Crochet hook, size G (4.00 mm) **or** size needed for gauge
Yarn needle

GAUGE: Each Square = 6"

Gauge Swatch: 2¼"
Work same as Square through Rnd 3.

SQUARE (Make 80)
With Brown, ch 5; join with slip st to form a ring.
Rnd 1 (Wrong side): Ch 1, (3 sc, tr) 4 times in ring; join with slip st to first sc: 16 sts.
Rnd 2: Ch 1, sc in same st, tr in next sc, sc in next sc, (tr, sc, tr) in next tr, ★ sc in next sc, tr in next sc, sc in next sc, (tr, sc, tr) in next tr; repeat from ★ around; join with slip st to first sc: 24 sts.
Note: Loop a short piece of yarn around **back** of any stitch on Rnd 1 to mark **right** side.

Rnd 3: Ch 1, sc in same st and in next 3 sts, (sc, tr, sc) in next sc, ★ sc in next 5 sts, (sc, tr, sc) in next sc; repeat from ★ 2 times **more**, sc in last tr; join with slip st to first sc, finish off: 32 sts.
Note: Begin working in rows.
Row 1: With **wrong** side facing and working across 2 sides only, join Gold with slip st in any tr; ch 1, sc in same st, tr in next sc, (sc in next sc, tr in next sc) 3 times, (sc, tr) in next tr, changing to Tan in last tr *(Fig. 22a, page 125)*, (tr, sc) in same st, place marker around last tr made, (tr in next st, sc in next st) 4 times: 10 sts **each** side.
Row 2: Ch 1, turn; sc in each st across to marked tr, 2 sc in marked tr changing to Gold in last sc, sc in next tr, place marker around last sc made, sc in same st as last sc and in each st across: 11 sts **each** side.
Row 3: Ch 1, turn; sc in first sc, tr in next sc, (sc in next sc, tr in next sc) across to marked sc, (sc, tr) in marked sc changing to Tan in last tr, (tr, sc) in next sc, place marker around last tr made, (tr in next sc, sc in next sc) across: 12 sts **each** side.
Rows 4-6: Repeat Rows 2 and 3 once, then repeat Row 2 once **more**: 15 sts **each** side.
Row 7: Ch 1, turn; sc in first sc, tr in next sc, (sc in next sc, tr in next sc) across to marked sc, (sc, tr) in marked sc changing to Tan in last tr; cut Gold, (tr, sc) in next sc, place marker around last tr made, (tr in next sc, sc in next sc) across changing to Lt Teal in last sc; cut Tan: 16 sts **each** side.
Row 8: Ch 1, turn; sc in each st across to marked tr, 2 sc in marked tr changing to Teal in last sc, sc in next tr, place marker around last sc made, sc in same st as last sc and in each st across: 17 sts **each** side.
Row 9: Ch 1, turn; sc in first sc, tr in next sc, (sc in next sc, tr in next sc) across to marked sc, (sc, tr) in marked sc changing to Lt Teal in last tr, (tr, sc) in next sc, place marker around last tr made, (tr in next sc, sc in next sc) across: 18 sts **each** side.
Rows 10-13: Repeat Rows 8 and 9 twice: 22 sts **each** side.
Row 14: Ch 1, turn; sc in each st across to marked tr, 2 sc in marked tr changing to Teal in last sc; cut Lt Teal, 2 sc in next tr, sc in each st across; finish off leaving a long end for sewing: 23 sts **each** side.

ASSEMBLY
With yarn end, using Placement Diagram, page 104, as a guide, and working in end of rows and in both loops of stitches, whipstitch Squares together *(Fig. 26b, page 126)*, forming 8 vertical strips of 10 Squares each; using Teal, whipstitch strips together in same manner.

Instructions continued on page 104.

TRUE BLUE FRIEND

When the going gets tough for someone close to you, show that you'll always be a "true blue friend" with this lacy mile-a-minute afghan.

LACY MILE-A-MINUTE

Finished Size: 46" x 64"

MATERIALS
Worsted Weight Yarn:
32 ounces, (910 grams, 2,195 yards)
Crochet hook, size I (5.50 mm) **or** size needed for gauge

GAUGE: In pattern, (sc, ch 3) 6 times = 4"
Each Strip = 5¾" wide

Gauge Swatch: 4"w x 10"h
Ch 16 **loosely.**
Work same as First Strip through Rnd 4.
Finish off.

STITCH GUIDE

PICOT
Ch 3, slip st in top of st just made *(Fig. 25, page 126)*.

FIRST STRIP
Ch 168 **loosely.**

Rnd 1 (Right side): (Sc, ch 3) 3 times in second ch from hook, (skip next ch, sc in next ch, ch 3) across, sc in same st, ch 3, place marker around last ch-3 made for st placement, (sc in same st, ch 3) twice; working in free loops of beginning ch *(Fig. 21b, page 125)*, skip next ch, (sc in next ch, ch 3, skip next ch) across, sc in same st as first sc, ch 3; join with slip st to first sc: 172 ch-3 sps.
Note: Loop a short piece of yarn around any stitch to mark Rnd 1 as **right** side.

Rnd 2: Slip st in first ch-3 sp, ch 3, (dc, ch 3, 2 dc) in same sp, ch 3, 2 dc in next ch-3 sp, ch 3, ★ skip next ch-3 sp, 2 dc in next ch-3 sp, ch 3; repeat from ★ across to marked ch-3 sp, (2 dc, ch 3, 2 dc) in marked ch-3 sp, place marker around ch-3 just made for st placement, ch 3, 2 dc in next ch-3 sp, ch 3, (skip next ch-3 sp, 2 dc in next ch-3 sp, ch 3) across; join with slip st to top of beginning ch-3: 90 ch-3 sps.

Rnd 3: Slip st in next dc and in next ch-3 sp, ch 1, 5 sc in same sp, ch 4, (3 sc in next ch-3 sp, ch 4) across to marked ch-3 sp, 5 sc in marked ch-3 sp, ch 4, (3 sc in next ch-3 sp, ch 4) across; join with slip st to first sc: 274 sc and 90 ch-4 sps.

Rnd 4: Ch 4 (**counts as first dc plus ch 1**), dc in next sc, ch 1, † (tr, ch 1, tr) in next sc, (ch 1, dc in next sc) twice, sc in next ch-4 sp, ★ dc in next sc, (ch 1, dc in next sc) twice, sc in next ch-4 sp; repeat from ★ across to next 5-sc group †, (dc in next sc, ch 1) twice, repeat from † to † once; join with slip st to first dc: 186 ch-1 sps.

Rnd 5: Slip st in first ch-1 sp, ch 1, sc in same sp, † ch 2, sc in next ch-1 sp, ch 2, 3 dc in next ch-1 sp, (ch 2, sc in next ch-1 sp) twice, skip next dc, (dc, ch 3, dc) in next sc, ★ sc in next ch-1 sp, ch 1, sc in next ch-1 sp, skip next dc, (dc, ch 3, dc) in next sc; repeat from ★ 43 times **more** †, sc in next ch-1 sp, repeat from † to † once; join with slip st to first sc.

Rnd 6: Slip st in first ch-2 sp, ch 1, sc in same sp, work Picot, ch 1, sc in next ch-2 sp, work Picot, ch 1, † (dc, ch 1) twice in next dc, tr in next dc, work Picot, ch 1, (dc, ch 1) twice in next dc, (sc in next ch-2 sp, work Picot, ch 1) twice, (sc, ch 3, sc) in next ch-3 sp, 3 dc in next ch-1 sp, (dc, ch 3, dc) in next ch-3 sp, ★ dc in next ch-1 sp, (dc, ch 3, dc) in next ch-3 sp; repeat from ★ 41 times **more**, 3 dc in next ch-1 sp, (sc, ch 3, sc) in next ch-3 sp, ch 1 †, (sc in next ch-2 sp, work Picot, ch 1) twice, repeat from † to † once; join with slip st to first sc, finish off.

Instructions continued on page 104.

LITTLE ANGEL

Made for my daughter Giovanna, this rosy gift set says "Thank heaven for little girls!" Pink blooms enhance the lacy afghan, and a golden-haired guardian will keep watch as baby blossoms.

ANGEL DOLL

Finished Size: Approximately 4½" tall and 7½" wide

MATERIALS
Sport Weight Yarn:
Peach for Head - 20 yards
Black for eyes - small amount
Brushed Acrylic for Hair - 35 yards
Pompadour for Collar and Wings
White - 35 yards
Pink - 15 yards
Crochet hook, size B (2.25 mm) **or** size needed
for gauge
⅛"w Ribbon - 24" length
Polyester fiberfill

GAUGE: 12 sc and 12 rows = 2"

Gauge Swatch: 2" square
Ch 13 **loosely**.
Row 1: Sc in second ch from hook and in each ch across.
Rows 2-12: Ch 1, turn; sc in each sc across.
Finish off.

STITCH GUIDE

SC DECREASE
Pull up a loop in next 2 sc, YO and draw through all 3 loops on hook (**counts as one sc**).

DC DECREASE (uses next 2 sts)
★ YO, insert hook in **next** dc, YO and pull up a loop, YO and draw through 2 loops on hook; repeat from ★ once **more**, YO and draw through all 3 loops on hook (**counts as one dc**).
BEGINNING CLUSTER (uses one st or sp)
Ch 2, dc in same st or sp.
CLUSTER (uses one st or sp)
★ YO, insert hook in st or sp indicated, YO and pull up a loop, YO and draw through 2 loops on hook; repeat from ★ once **more**, YO and draw through all 3 loops on hook (**Figs. 16a & b, page 124**).

HEAD
Rnd 1 (Right side)**:** Beginning at top with Peach, ch 2, 8 sc in second ch from hook; join with slip st to first sc.
Rnd 2: Ch 1, 2 sc in same st and in each sc around; join with slip st to first sc: 16 sc.
Rnd 3: Ch 1, sc in same st, 2 sc in next sc, (sc in next sc, 2 sc in next sc) around; join with slip st to first sc: 24 sc.
Rnd 4: Ch 1, sc in same st and in next sc, 2 sc in next sc, (sc in next 2 sc, 2 sc in next sc) around; join with slip st to first sc: 32 sc.
Rnds 5-15: Ch 1, sc in same st and in each sc around; join with slip st to first sc.
Rnd 16: Ch 1, sc in same st, skip next sc, (sc in next sc, skip next sc) around; join with slip st to first sc: 16 sc.
Rnd 17: Ch 1, sc in same st and in each sc around; join with slip st to Back Loop Only of first sc (**Fig. 20, page 125**).
Stuff Head firmly with polyester fiberfill.
Rnd 18: Ch 1, working in Back Loops Only, sc decrease around; join with slip st to **both** loops of first sc: 8 sc.
Rnd 19: Ch 1, working in both loops, sc decrease around; join with slip st to first sc, finish off.
Using photo as a guide for placement, add French knot eyes allowing needle to pass between Rnds 9 and 10 (**Fig. 32, page 127**).

COLLAR
Rnd 1 (Right side)**:** With top of Head toward you and working in free loops on Rnd 17 (**Fig. 21a, page 125**), join White with slip st in any sc; ch 3 (**counts as first dc, now and throughout**), 2 dc in same st, 3 dc in each sc around; join with slip st to first dc: 48 dc.
Rnd 2: Ch 3, dc in next dc and in each dc around; join with slip st to first dc.
Rnd 3: Work beginning Cluster, ch 2, dc in second ch from hook, work Cluster in same st as beginning Cluster, skip next 3 dc, ★ work Cluster in next dc, ch 2, dc in second ch from hook, work Cluster in same st as last Cluster made, skip next 3 dc; repeat from ★ around; join with slip st to top of beginning Cluster; do **not** finish off: 24 Clusters.

Instructions continued on page 26.

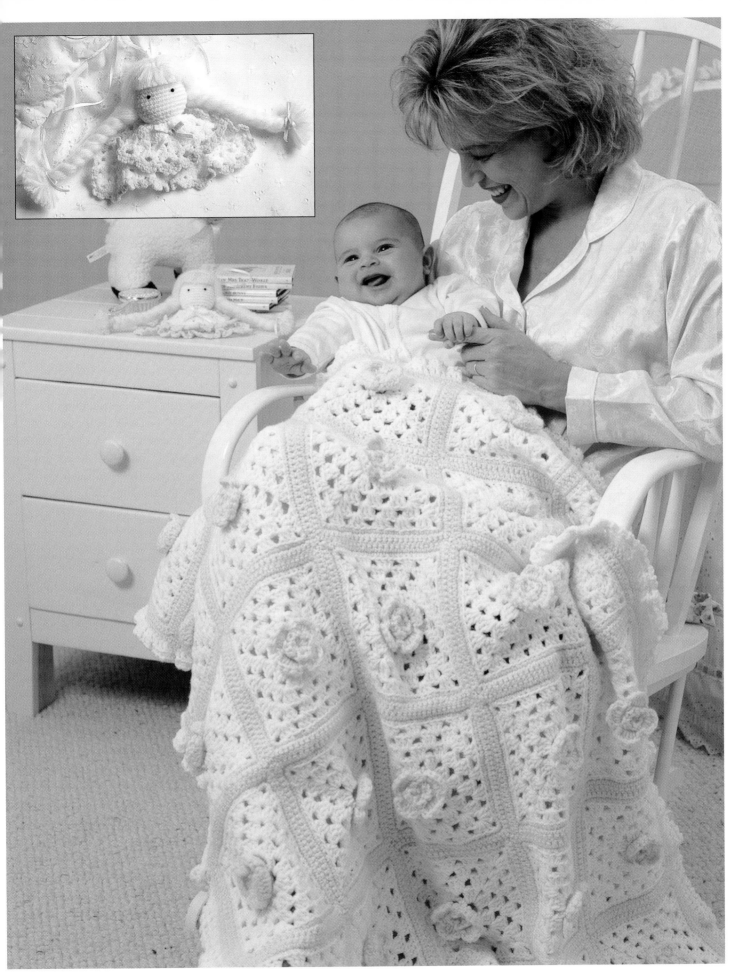

Rnd 4: Work beginning Cluster, ch 4, work Cluster in same st, skip next Cluster, ★ work (Cluster, ch 4, Cluster) in next Cluster, skip next Cluster; repeat from ★ around; join with slip st to top of beginning Cluster, finish off: 12 ch-4 sps.

Rnd 5: With **right** side facing, join Pink with sc in ch-4 sp at center back (*see Joining With Sc, page 125*); ch 3, (sc in same sp, ch 3) 4 times, (sc, ch 3) 5 times in each ch-4 sp around; join with slip st to first sc, finish off.

HAIR
BANGS
Cut nineteen 2½" lengths of yarn. Using photo as a guide for placement, and working around sc on Rnds 2 and 4, fold one strand in half and draw the folded end around an sc, pull the loose ends through the folded end (*Fig. 1*). Trim to desired length.

Fig. 1

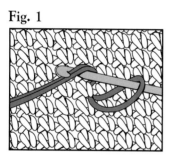

BRAIDS
Ch 16 **loosely**; finish off.
Holding 2 strands of yarn together, add 9" fringe (*Figs. 27a & b, page 126*) in top and bottom loop along sides of ch-16 (*Figs. 2a & b*).
Working through back ridge of ch (*Fig. 2b, page 122*), sew to center of Head from front to back, having one end flush against Bangs.
Pull hair into a ponytail on each side; tie and sew to Head between Rnds 11 and 12. Braid ponytails, secure ends, and trim.
Tie one 9" length of ribbon in a bow around end of each ponytail; trim as desired.

Fig. 2a

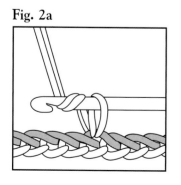

Fig. 2b

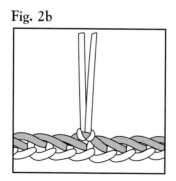

WINGS
FIRST SIDE
With White, ch 10; join with slip st to form a ring.
Row 1: Ch 3, 11 dc in ring: 12 dc.
Row 2 (Right side): Ch 2, turn; dc in next dc and in each dc across to last 2 dc, dc decrease: 10 dc.
Note: Loop a short piece of yarn around any stitch to mark Row 2 as **right** side.
Rows 3-5: Ch 2, turn; dc in next dc and in each dc across to last 2 dc, dc decrease: 4 dc.
Row 6: Ch 2, turn; dc in next dc, dc decrease: 2 dc.
Row 7: Ch 2, turn; dc in last dc; finish off: one dc.

SECOND SIDE
Row 1: With **wrong** side facing, join White with slip st in ring; ch 3, 11 dc in ring: 12 dc.
Rows 2-7: Work same as First Side; do **not** finish off.

EDGING
Rnd 1: Ch 1, turn; sc in last dc worked on Row 7 of Second Side, † ch 3, working across end of rows, sc in top of dc on Row 6, ch 3, (sc in top of dc on next row, ch 3) 5 times, sc in top of dc on Row 1 of next side, ch 3, (sc in top of dc on next row, ch 3) 6 times †, sc in same st, repeat from † to † once; join with slip st to first sc: 28 ch-3 sps.
Rnd 2: Slip st in first ch-3 sp, work (beginning Cluster, ch 3, Cluster) in same sp, work (Cluster, ch 3, Cluster) in each ch-3 sp around; join with slip st to top of beginning Cluster, finish off.
Rnd 3: With **right** side facing, join Pink with sc in any ch-3 sp; ch 3, (sc in same sp, ch 3) twice, (sc, ch 3) 3 times in each ch-3 sp around; join with slip st to first sc, finish off.

Tack Wings to back of angel.
Tie remaining ribbon in a bow and attach to center front of Collar.

ANGELIC BLOSSOMS

Finished Size: 36" x 42"

MATERIALS
Worsted Weight Yarn:
    White - 16 ounces, (450 grams, 1,095 yards)
    Pink - 12½ ounces, (360 grams, 860 yards)
Crochet hook, size G (4.00 mm) **or** size needed for gauge
Yarn needle

GAUGE SWATCH: Each Square = 6½"

STITCH GUIDE

> **BACK POST SINGLE CROCHET**
> *(abbreviated BPsc)*
> Insert hook from **back** to **front** around post of st indicated *(Fig. 13, page 124)*, YO and pull up a loop, YO and draw through both loops on hook.

SQUARE (Make 30)
With Pink, ch 4; join with slip st to form a ring.
Rnd 1 (Right side): Ch 3 **(counts as first dc, now and throughout)**, (2 dc, slip st) in ring, (3 dc, slip st) 3 times in ring; join with slip st to first dc: 4 3-dc groups.
Note: Loop a short piece of yarn around any stitch to mark Rnd 1 as **right** side.
Rnd 2: Ch 1, work BPsc around next dc, ch 3, ★ work BPsc around center dc of next 3-dc group, ch 3; repeat from ★ 2 times **more**; join with slip st to first BPsc: 4 ch-3 sps.
Rnd 3: (Slip st, 5 dc, slip st) in each ch-3 sp around; do **not** join.
Rnd 4: Ch 1, work BPsc around first BPsc on Rnd 2, ch 5, ★ work BPsc around next BPsc on Rnd 2, ch 5; repeat from ★ 2 times **more**; join with slip st to first BPsc, finish off: 4 ch-5 sps.
Rnd 5: With **right** side facing, and working in ch-5 sps **behind** Rnd 3, join White with slip st in any ch-5 sp; ch 3, 2 dc in same sp, ch 1, ★ (3 dc, ch 2, 3 dc) in next ch-5 sp, ch 1; repeat from ★ 2 times **more**, 3 dc in same sp as first dc, ch 1, sc in first dc to form last ch-2 sp: 24 dc and 8 sps.
Rnd 6: Ch 3, 2 dc in same sp, ch 1, 3 dc in next ch-1 sp, ch 1, ★ (3 dc, ch 2, 3 dc) in next ch-2 sp, ch 1, 3 dc in next ch-1 sp, ch 1; repeat from ★ 2 times **more**, 3 dc in same sp as first dc, ch 1, sc in first dc to form last ch-2 sp: 36 dc and 12 sps.
Rnds 7 and 8: Ch 3, 2 dc in same sp, ch 1, (3 dc in next ch-1 sp, ch 1) across to next corner ch-2 sp, ★ (3 dc, ch 2, 3 dc) in corner ch-2 sp, ch 1, (3 dc in next ch-1 sp, ch 1) across to next corner ch-2 sp; repeat from ★ 2 times **more**, 3 dc in same sp as first dc, ch 1, sc in first dc to form last ch-2 sp: 60 dc and 20 sps.
Finish off.

Rnd 9: With **right** side facing, join Pink with sc in any corner ch-2 sp *(see Joining With Sc, page 125)*; 2 sc in same sp, sc in Back Loop Only of each dc and each ch across to next corner ch-2 sp *(Fig. 20, page 125)*, ★ 5 sc in corner ch-2 sp, sc in Back Loop Only of each dc and each ch across to next corner ch-2 sp; repeat from ★ 2 times **more**, 2 sc in same sp as first sc; join with slip st to **both** loops of first sc: 96 sc.
Rnd 10: Ch 1, **turn**; working in both loops, 2 sc in same st, sc in each sc across to center sc of next corner 5-sc group, ★ 3 sc in center sc, sc in each sc across to center sc of next corner 5-sc group; repeat from ★ 2 times **more**, sc in same st as first sc; join with slip st to first sc, finish off: 104 sc.

ASSEMBLY
With Pink and working through both loops, whipstitch Squares together *(Fig. 26b, page 126)*, forming 5 vertical strips of 6 Squares each, beginning in center sc of first corner 3-sc group and ending in center sc of next corner 3-sc group; whipstitch strips together in same manner.

EDGING
Rnd 1: With **right** side facing, join Pink with sc in center sc of any corner 3-sc group; sc in same st, ★ † sc in next 25 sc, (sc in same st as joining on same Square and in same st as joining on next Square, sc in next 25 sc) across to center sc of next corner 3-sc group †, 3 sc in center sc; repeat from ★ 2 times **more**, then repeat from † to † once, sc in same st as first sc; join with slip st to first sc: 598 sc.
Rnd 2: Ch 1, **turn**; 2 sc in same st, sc in each sc around working 3 sc in center sc of each corner 3-sc group, sc in same st as first sc; join with slip st to first sc, finish off: 606 sc.
Rnd 3: With **right** side facing and working in Back Loops Only, join White with slip st in center sc of any corner 3-sc group; ch 4, dc in same st, ch 1, (dc in next sc, ch 1) around working (dc, ch 1) twice in center sc of each corner 3-sc group; join with slip st to third ch of beginning ch-4.
Rnd 4: Ch 1, working in Back Loops Only, sc in same st, ch 2, (sc in next dc, ch 2) around; join with slip st to **both** loops of first sc, finish off.

MOTHER'S DAY

Honor Mother on her special day with a flowered throw that's embellished with bouquets of violets, symbols of love and devotion.

VIOLETS IN BLOOM

Finished Size: 40" x 65"

MATERIALS
Worsted Weight Brushed Acrylic Yarn:
  Off-White - 48 ounces, (1,360 grams, 2,430 yards)
  Violet - 7 ounces, (200 grams, 355 yards)
  Green - 1½ ounces, (40 grams, 75 yards)
  Yellow - ½ ounce, (15 grams, 25 yards)
Crochet hook, size G (4.00 mm) **or** size needed for gauge
Yarn needle
Safety pin

GAUGE: 17 sc and 18 rows = 5"
Each Square, Rows 1-35 = 9¾" square

Gauge Swatch: 5" square
With Off-White, ch 18 **loosely.**
Work same as Square through Row 18: 17 sc.
Finish off.

SQUARE (Make 15)
With Off-White, ch 34 **loosely.**
Row 1 (Right side): Sc in second ch from hook and in each ch across: 33 sc.
Note: Loop a short piece of yarn around any stitch to mark Row 1 as **right** side and bottom edge.
Rows 2-35: Ch 1, turn; sc in each sc across; do **not** finish off.

BORDER
Rnd 1: Ch 3 (**counts as first dc, now and throughout**), (dc, ch 2, 2 dc) in same st, work 31 dc evenly spaced across end of rows; working in free loops of beginning ch (*Fig. 21b, page 125*), (2 dc, ch 2, 2 dc) in first ch, dc in each ch across to last ch, (2 dc, ch 2, 2 dc) in last ch; work 31 dc evenly spaced across end of rows; working across last row, (2 dc, ch 2, 2 dc) in first sc, dc in each sc across; join with slip st to first dc: 140 dc.
Rnd 2: Ch 4, skip next dc, (2 dc, ch 2, 2 dc) in next corner ch-2 sp, ★ ch 1, skip next dc, (dc in next dc, ch 1, skip next dc) across to next corner ch-2 sp, (2 dc, ch 2, 2 dc) in corner ch-2 sp; repeat from ★ 2 times **more**, ch 1, skip next dc, (dc in next dc, ch 1, skip next dc) across; join with slip st to third ch of beginning ch-4: 84 dc and 76 sps.
Rnd 3: Ch 3, dc in next ch-1 sp and in next 2 dc, (2 dc, ch 2, 2 dc) in next corner ch-2 sp, ★ dc in each dc and in each ch-1 sp across to next corner ch-2 sp, (2 dc, ch 2, 2 dc) in corner ch-2 sp; repeat from ★ 2 times **more**, dc in each dc and in each ch-1 sp across; join with slip st to first dc, finish off: 172 dc.

CHAIN
Holding 2 strands of Violet together, chain a 44" length; do **not** finish off, slip loop from hook onto safety pin. Weave beginning end of chain through Rnd 2 of Border, working through ch-1 sps along sides and dc at corners; remove loop from safety pin and slip onto hook; adjust length as needed, join with slip st to first st, finish off.

FINISHING
Work embroidery on 7 Squares, following Chart, page 105.

ASSEMBLY
Use photo as a guide for placement, alternate plain and cross-stitched Squares, placing bottom edges at the same end. With Off-White and working through both loops, whipstitch Squares together (*Fig. 26b, page 126*), forming 3 vertical strips of 5 Squares each; whipstitch strips together in same manner, securing seam at each joining.

EDGING
With **right** side facing, join Off-White with slip st in any corner ch-2 sp; ch 3, (dc, ch 2, 2 dc) in same sp, ★ † dc in each dc across Square, [dc in next ch-2 sp, dc in next joining and in next ch-2 sp, dc in each dc across Square] across to next corner ch-2 sp †, (2 dc, ch 2, 2 dc) in corner ch-2 sp; repeat from ★ 2 times **more**, then repeat from † to † once; join with slip st to first dc, finish off.

Holding 6 strands of Off-White together, add 6" fringe evenly across short edges of Afghan (*Figs. 27a & b, page 126*).

FATHER'S DAY

For a Father's Day delight, surprise Dad with this bold wrap. Its rugged Bear's Paw motifs evoke the manly comforts of an evening at the lodge.

BEAR'S PAW

Finished Size: 50" x 66"

MATERIALS
Worsted Weight Yarn:
    Grey - 30 ounces, (850 grams, 2,055 yards)
    Burgundy - 14½ ounces, (410 grams, 995 yards)
Crochet hook, size G (4.00 mm) **or** size needed for gauge
Yarn needle

GAUGE SWATCH: 2¾"
Work same as Square A or Square B.

STITCH GUIDE

BEGINNING DECREASE
Pull up a loop in first 2 sc, YO and draw through all 3 loops on hook (**counts as one sc**).
ENDING DECREASE
Pull up a loop in last 2 sc, YO and draw through all 3 loops on hook (**counts as one sc**).

SQUARE A
Note: Make the number of Squares indicated with the following colors: Grey - 197, Burgundy - 94.
Ch 4; join with slip st to form a ring.
Rnd 1 (Right side): Ch 5 (**counts as first dc plus ch 2, now and throughout**), (3 dc in ring, ch 2) 3 times, 2 dc in ring; join with slip st to first dc: 12 dc and 4 ch-2 sps.

Note: Loop a short piece of yarn around any stitch to mark Rnd 1 as **right** side.
Rnd 2: Slip st in first ch-2 sp, ch 3 (**counts as first dc, now and throughout**), (2 dc, ch 2, 3 dc) in same sp, ch 1, ★ (3 dc, ch 2, 3 dc) in next ch-2 sp, ch 1; repeat from ★ 2 times **more**; join with slip st to first dc, finish off: 24 dc and 8 sps.

SQUARE B (Make 100)
With Grey, ch 4; join with slip st to form a ring.
Rnd 1 (Right side): Ch 5, 3 dc in ring, cut Grey, with Burgundy, YO and draw through, ch 1, 3 dc in ring, ch 2, 3 dc in ring, cut Burgundy, with Grey, YO and draw through, ch 1, 2 dc in ring; join with slip st to first dc: 12 dc and 4 sps.
Note: Mark Rnd 1 as **right** side.
Rnd 2: Slip st in first ch-2 sp, ch 3, (2 dc, ch 2, 3 dc) in same sp, ch 1, 3 dc in next ch-2 sp, cut Grey, with Burgundy, YO and draw through, ch 1, 3 dc in same sp, ch 1, (3 dc, ch 2, 3 dc) in next ch-2 sp, ch 1, 3 dc in next ch-2 sp, cut Burgundy, with Grey, YO and draw through, ch 1, 3 dc in same sp, ch 1; join with slip st to first dc, finish off: 24 dc and 8 sps.

ASSEMBLY
With matching color, using photo and Placement Diagram as a guide, and working through inside loops only, whipstitch Squares together (**Fig. 26a, page 126**), forming 17 vertical strips of 23 Squares each, beginning in second ch of first corner ch-2 and ending in first ch of next corner ch-2; whipstitch strips together in same manner.

PLACEMENT DIAGRAM

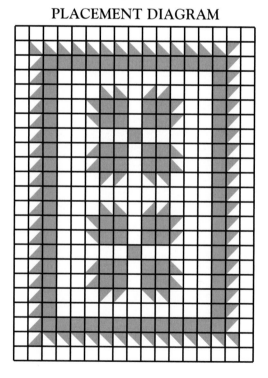

Instructions continued on page 105.

SCHOOL SPIRIT

Whether they're in high school or going away to college, students will cheer for this mile-a-minute coverlet. It's striped with team colors that will be at home at the stadium or in the dorm.

TRACK AND FIELD

Finished Size: 48" x 64"

MATERIALS
Worsted Weight Yarn:
   Blue - 29 ounces, (820 grams, 1,825 yards)
   Yellow - 23 ounces, (650 grams, 1,445 yards)
Crochet hook, size G (4.00 mm) **or** size needed
   for gauge
Yarn needle

GAUGE: 16 dc and 8 rows = 4"
   Each Strip = 4" wide

Gauge Swatch: 4" square
Ch 18 **loosely.**
Row 1: Dc in fourth ch from hook **(3 skipped chs count as first dc)** and in each ch across: 16 dc.
Rows 2-8: Ch 3 **(counts as first dc)**, turn; dc in next dc and in each dc across.
Finish off.

STRIP (Make 12)
CENTER
Note: Center will measure approximately 49".
With Blue, ch 9 **loosely.**
Row 1: Dc in fourth ch from hook **(3 skipped chs count as first dc)** and in next ch, ch 1, skip next ch, dc in last 3 chs: 6 dc.

Row 2 (Right side): Ch 3 **(counts as first dc, now and throughout)**, turn; working in Back Loops Only **(Fig. 20, page 125)**, dc in next 2 dc, ch 1, dc in last 3 dc.
*Note: Loop a short piece of yarn around any stitch to mark Row 2 as **right** side and bottom edge.*
Row 3: Ch 3, turn; working in Front Loops Only, dc in next 2 dc, ch 1, dc in last 3 dc.
Row 4: Ch 3, turn; working in Back Loops Only, dc in next 2 dc, ch 1, dc in last 3 dc.
Rows 5-98: Repeat Rows 3 and 4, 47 times.
Finish off.

BORDER
Note #1: Center will not lie flat until Rnd 2 is completed.
Note #2: At completion of Rnd 1, Strip should measure approximately 61".
Rnd 1: With **right** side facing and working in both loops, join Yellow with slip st in first dc on Row 98; ch 3, (2 dc, slip st) in same st, (3 dc, slip st) in next ch-1 sp, skip next 2 dc, (3 dc, slip st) in last dc and in end of each row across; working in free loops of beginning ch **(Fig. 21b, page 125)**, (3 dc, slip st) in ch at base of first dc and in next sp, skip next 2 chs, (3 dc, slip st) in last ch and in end of each row across; join with slip st to first dc, finish off: 606 dc.
Rnd 2: With **right** side facing and working in Back Loops Only, join Blue with sc in center dc of first 3-dc group **(see Joining With Sc, page 125)**; ch 2, skip next 2 dc, (sc in next dc, ch 2, skip next 2 dc) around; join with slip st to Back Loop Only of first sc: 202 sc.
Rnd 3: Ch 3, working in Back Loop Only of each sc and each ch, dc in same st, 2 dc in each of next 7 sts, dc in next 294 sts, 2 dc in each of next 9 sts, dc in next ch and in each st across to last ch, 2 dc in last ch changing to Yellow in last dc **(Fig. 22a, page 125)**; join with slip st to first dc: 624 dc.
Rnd 4: Ch 1, working in Back Loops Only, sc in same st and in next 16 dc, † place marker around last sc made for joining placement, sc in next 293 dc, place marker around last sc made for joining placement †, sc in next 19 dc, repeat from † to † once, sc in last 2 dc; join with slip st to **both** loops of first sc, finish off.

ASSEMBLY
Place two Strips together with bottom edges at the same end. With Yellow and working through inside loops only, whipstitch Strips together **(Fig. 26a, page 126)**, beginning in first marked sc and ending in next marked sc. Join remaining Strips in same manner, always working in same direction.

I'M SO BLUE WITHOUT YOU

To me, a handmade gift is the best way to reach across the miles and touch the heart of a faraway friend. The waterfall look of this ripple design says, "I'm so blue without you!"

WATERFALL RIPPLE

Finished Size: 44" x 62"

MATERIALS
Worsted Weight Yarn:
  Lt Blue - 10 ounces, (280 grams, 655 yards)
  Blue - 10 ounces, (280 grams, 655 yards)
  Med Blue - 10 ounces, (280 grams, 655 yards)
  Dk Blue - 6 ounces, (170 grams, 395 yards)
  White - 5 ounces, (140 grams, 330 yards)
Crochet hook, size H (5.00 mm) **or** size needed
  for gauge

GAUGE: Each repeat from point to point = 5¹/₂";
        6 rows = 4¹/₂"

Gauge Swatch: 11"w x 4¹/₂"h
Ch 50 **loosely.**
Work same as Afghan for 6 rows.
Finish off.

STITCH GUIDE

BEGINNING CLUSTER (uses first 3 sts)
Ch 2, turn; ★ YO, insert hook in **next** st, YO and pull up a loop, YO and draw through 2 loops on hook; repeat from ★ once **more**, YO and draw through all 3 loops on hook *(Figs. 17a & b, page 124).*

CLUSTER (uses next 5 sts)
★ YO, insert hook in **next** st, YO and pull up a loop, YO and draw through 2 loops on hook; repeat from ★ 4 times **more**, YO and draw through all 6 loops on hook.
ENDING CLUSTER (uses last 3 sts)
★ YO, insert hook in **next** st, YO and pull up a loop, YO and draw through 2 loops on hook; repeat from ★ 2 times **more**, YO and draw through all 4 loops on hook.
LONG FRONT POST TREBLE CROCHET
  (abbreviated LFPtr)
YO twice, insert hook from **front** to **back** *(Fig. 10, page 123)* around post of dc one row **below** next dc, YO and pull up a loop even with last st made, (YO and draw through 2 loops on hook) 3 times. Skip dc behind LFPtr.

COLOR SEQUENCE
2 Rows **each:** Dk Blue, ★ Med Blue, Blue, Lt Blue, White, Lt Blue, Blue, Med Blue, Dk Blue; repeat from ★ throughout *(Fig. 22a, page 125).*

AFGHAN
With Dk Blue, ch 194 **loosely.**
Row 1 (Right side)**:** YO, insert hook in third ch from hook, YO and pull up a loop, YO and draw through 2 loops on hook, YO, insert hook in next ch, YO and pull up a loop, YO and draw through 2 loops on hook, YO and draw through all 3 loops on hook, dc in next 9 chs, 5 dc in next ch, dc in next 9 chs, ★ work Cluster, dc in next 9 chs, 5 dc in next ch, dc in next 9 chs; repeat from ★ across to last 3 chs, work ending Cluster: 193 sts.
Row 2: Work beginning Cluster, dc in next 9 dc, 5 dc in next dc, dc in next 9 dc, ★ work Cluster, dc in next 9 dc, 5 dc in next dc, dc in next 9 dc; repeat from ★ across to last 3 sts, work ending Cluster.
Row 3: Work beginning Cluster, dc in next 5 dc, work LFPtr, dc in next 3 dc, 5 dc in next dc, dc in next 3 dc, work LFPtr, dc in next 5 dc, ★ work Cluster, dc in next 5 dc, work LFPtr, dc in next 3 dc, 5 dc in next dc, dc in next 3 dc, work LFPtr, dc in next 5 dc; repeat from ★ across to last 3 sts, work ending Cluster.
Row 4: Work beginning Cluster, dc in next 9 sts, 5 dc in next dc, dc in next 9 sts, ★ work Cluster, dc in next 9 sts, 5 dc in next dc, dc in next 9 sts; repeat from ★ across to last 3 sts, work ending Cluster.
Repeat Rows 3 and 4 until Afghan measures approximately 62" from beginning ch, ending by working 2 rows Dk Blue; finish off.

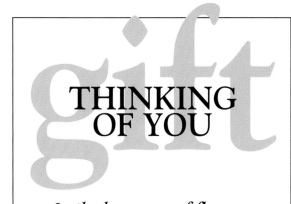

THINKING OF YOU

In the language of flowers, pansies symbolize love and kind thoughts. You'll want to make this wrap for someone who's important in your life.

PRETTY PANSIES

Finished Size: 52" x 69"

MATERIALS
Worsted Weight Yarn:
    Green - 37 ounces, (1,050 grams, 2,535 yards)
    Dk Green - 9 ounces, (260 grams, 615 yards)
    Lt Blue - 1 ounce, (30 grams, 70 yards)
    Blue - 1 ounce, (30 grams, 70 yards)
    Lt Purple - 1 ounce, (30 grams, 70 yards)
    Purple - 1 ounce, (30 grams, 70 yards)
    Rose - 1 ounce, (30 grams, 70 yards)
    Black - 1 ounce, (30 grams, 70 yards)
    Yellow - 10 yards
Crochet hooks, sizes G (4.00 mm) **and** H (5.00 mm)
    or sizes needed for gauge
Yarn needle

GAUGE: Each Square B = 6¾"

Gauge Swatch: 3½" (top to bottom)
Work same as Square A Pansy.

STITCH GUIDE

DECREASE
Working to last dc of same Square at inside edge, YO, insert hook in last dc, YO and pull up a loop, YO, insert hook in first dc of next Square, YO and pull up a loop (5 loops on hook), YO and draw through all 5 loops on hook.

SQUARE A (Make 30)
Note: Make 6 Squares **each** using Lt Blue, Blue, Lt Purple, Purple, and Rose on Rnds 1 and 2 of Pansy.

PANSY
With small size hook and Black, ch 5; join with slip st to form a ring.
Foundation Row (Right side)**:** (Ch 3, 2 tr, ch 3, slip st) 3 times in ring; finish off.
Note: Loop a short piece of yarn around any stitch to mark Foundation Row as **right** side.
Rnd 1: With **right** side facing and small size hook, join color indicated with slip st in beginning ring; (ch 5, 4 tr tr, ch 5, slip st) twice in ring, ch 4, 4 tr in each of next 2 tr on Foundation Row, ch 4, (slip st in next slip st, ch 4, 4 tr in each of next 2 tr, ch 4) twice (Bottom Petals made); join with slip st to first slip st.
Rnd 2: Ch 2, † (slip st in next ch, ch 2) 5 times, working in Back Loops Only *(Fig. 20, page 125)*, (slip st in next tr tr, ch 2) 4 times, (slip st in next ch, ch 2) 5 times †, skip next slip st, repeat from † to † once (top Petals completed), slip st in next slip st, leave remaining sts unworked; finish off leaving a long end for sewing.
With Yellow, add 5 straight stitches to Black on center Bottom Petal of Foundation Row *(Fig. 30, page 127)*.

BACKGROUND
CIRCLE
Row 1 (Right side)**:** With large size hook and Dk Green, and leaving a long end for sewing, ch 6, 5 dc in sixth ch from hook **(5 skipped chs count as ch-5 sp)**, place marker around ch-5 for st placement.
Note: Mark Row 1 as **right** side.
Rows 2-16: Ch 5, turn; skip first 2 dc, 5 dc in next dc, leave remaining sts unworked.
Finish off.
With **wrong** side facing and using long end, sew ch at base of 5-dc group on Row 1 to center dc of 5-dc group on Row 16 to form a circle.

INSIDE
Rnd 1: With **right** side facing and large size hook, join Dk Green with sc in any ch-5 sp on inside of Circle *(see Joining With Sc, page 125)*; ch 2, (sc in next ch-5 sp, ch 2) 7 times; join with slip st to first sc: 8 sc and 8 ch-2 sps.
Rnd 2: Ch 1, sc in same st and in each sc around; join with slip st to first sc, finish off.

Instructions continued on page 105.

FOOTBALL FAN

Football fans will be ready for the big game with this reversible plaid afghan. The bright throw, along with snuggly mittens for him and her, will score lots of points at the stadium!

COZY MITTENS

Size:	Women's	Men's
Palm Circumference:	8"	9"
Hand Length:	7"	8"

Size Note: Instructions are written for Women's size with Men's size in braces. Instructions will be easier to read if you circle all the numbers pertaining to your size.

MATERIALS
Worsted Weight Yarn:
2³/₄{3¹/₂} ounces, [80{100} grams, 180{230} yards]
Crochet hook, size H (5.00 mm) **or** size needed for gauge
Yarn needle

GAUGE: In pattern, 4 sc and 4 rows = 1"

Gauge Swatch: 2" square
Ch 9 **loosely**.
Row 1: Sc in second ch from hook and in each ch across: 8 sc.
Rows 2-8: Ch 1, turn; sc in Back Loop Only of each sc across **(Fig. 20, page 125)**.
Finish off.

STITCH GUIDE

REVERSE SINGLE CROCHET
(abbreviated reverse sc)
Working from **left** to **right**, insert hook in sc to right of hook, YO and draw through, under, and to left of loop on hook (2 loops on hook), YO and draw through both loops on hook **(Figs. 19a-d, page 125)**.

MITTEN
Ch 81{89} **loosely**.
Note: Work in Back Loops Only throughout **(Fig. 20, page 125)**.
Row 1 (Right side): Sc in second ch from hook and in next 9 chs, slip st in next 5 chs, sc in next 23{27} chs, slip st in next 4 chs, sc in next 23{27} chs, slip st in next 5 chs, sc in last 10 chs: 80{88} sts.
Note: Loop a short piece of yarn around any stitch to mark Row 1 as **right** side.
Rows 2 thru 12{14}: Ch 1, turn; sc in first 10 sc, slip st in next 5 slip sts, sc in next 23{27} sc, slip st in next 4 slip sts, sc in next 23{27} sc, slip st in next 5 slip sts, sc in last 10 sc.
Row 13{15}: Ch 1, turn; sc in first 10 sc, slip st in next 5 slip sts, sc in next 9{11} sc, ch 17{21} (thumb), skip next 32{36} sts, sc in next 9{11} sc, slip st in next 5 slip sts, sc in last 10 sc: 48{52} sts.
Row 14{16}: Ch 1, turn; sc in first 10 sc, slip st in next 5 slip sts, sc in next 9{11} sc, sc in next 7{9} chs, slip st in next 3 chs, sc in next 7{9} chs, sc in next 9{11} sc, slip st in next 5 slip sts, sc in last 10 sc: 65{73} sts.
Rows 15{17} thru 17{19}: Ch 1, turn; sc in first 10 sc, slip st in next 5 slip sts, sc in next 35{43} sts, slip st in next 5 slip sts, sc in last 10 sc.
Finish off.

ASSEMBLY
With **right** sides together and matching sts, fold Mitten in half and whipstitch side and thumb edges together **(Fig. 26b, page 126)**, beginning in first sc and ending in last sc. Turn Mitten right side out.

EDGING
Rnd 1: With **right** side facing and working in end of rows; join yarn with slip st in last row, ch 1, sc in same row and in each row around; join with slip st to first sc.
Rnd 2: Ch 1, work reverse sc in each sc around; join with slip st to first st, finish off.

Instructions continued on page 106.

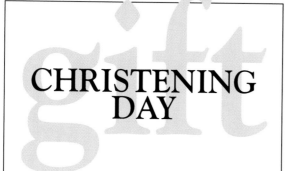

CHRISTENING DAY

To make your godchild's christening day even more memorable, create this delicate wrap. It will be treasured for a lifetime!

SWEET DREAMS

Finished Size: 36" x 45"

MATERIALS
Worsted Weight Yarn:
  37 ounces, (1,050 grams, 2,160 yards)
  Crochet hook, size G (4.00 mm) **or** size needed
   for gauge

GAUGE: In pattern, 7 5-dc groups = 5";
  11 rows = 4³/₄"

Gauge Swatch: 5¹/₂"w x 4³/₄"h
Ch 39 **loosely**.
Work same as Afghan Body for 11 rows.
Finish off.

AFGHAN BODY

Ch 224 **loosely**; place marker in third ch from hook for st placement.
Row 1 (Right side)**:** Dc in fourth ch from hook (**3 skipped chs count as first dc**), (ch 3, skip next 3 chs, dc in next 2 chs) across: 44 ch-3 sps.
Row 2: Ch 3 (**counts as first dc, now and throughout**), turn; 5 dc in center ch of each ch-3 across to last 2 dc, skip next dc, dc in last dc: 222 dc.
Row 3: Ch 3, turn; dc in next dc, (ch 3, skip next 3 dc, dc in next 2 dc) across: 44 ch-3 sps.
Repeat Rows 2 and 3 until Afghan Body measures approximately 41" from beginning ch, ending by working Row 3; do **not** finish off.

EDGING

Rnd 1: Ch 1, do **not** turn; 2 sc in last dc on last row; work 222 sc evenly spaced across end of rows; working in free loops of beginning ch (**Fig. 21b, page 125**), 3 sc in first ch, work 162 sc evenly spaced across to marked ch, 3 sc in marked ch; work 222 sc evenly spaced across end of rows; working in Back Loops Only across last row (**Fig. 20, page 125**), 3 sc in first dc, work 162 sc evenly spaced across, sc in same st as first sc; join with slip st to **both** loops of first sc: 780 sc.
Rnd 2: Ch 1, working in both loops, sc in same st, ch 5, skip next 4 sc, (sc in next sc, ch 5, skip next 4 sc) around; join with slip st to first sc: 156 ch-5 sps.
Rnd 3: Ch 1, sc in same st, ch 5, (sc in next sc, ch 5) around; join with slip st to first sc.
Rnd 4: Ch 1, sc in same st, ch 6, (sc in next sc, ch 6) around; join with slip st to first sc.
Rnd 5: Ch 1, sc in same st, ch 7, (sc in next sc, ch 7) around; join with slip st to first sc.
Rnd 6: Ch 1, sc in same st, ch 8, (sc in next sc, ch 8) around; join with slip st to first sc.
Rnd 7: Slip st in next 3 chs, ch 1, ★ (sc, ch 6, sc) around next loops of last 3 rnds, ch 6; repeat from ★ around; join with slip st to first sc, finish off.

TO MY HUSBAND WITH LOVE

*The classic argyle
pattern of this masculine
throw made it a handsome
gift for my husband,
George. He always
keeps it close by.*

CLASSIC ARGYLE

Finished Size: 56" x 72"

MATERIALS

Worsted Weight Yarn:
  Tan - 63 ounces, (1,790 grams, 3,870 yards)
  Blue - 14 ounces, (400 grams, 860 yards)
  Red - 5 ounces, (140 grams, 310 yards)
Crochet hook, size I (5.50 mm) **or** size needed for gauge
2 Bobbins
Yarn needle

GAUGE: 14 sc and 16 rows = 4"

Gauge Swatch: 4" square
Ch 15 **loosely**.
Row 1: Sc in second ch from hook and in each ch across: 14 sc.
Rows 2-16: Ch 1, turn; sc in each sc across.
Finish off.

STITCH GUIDE

> **FRONT POST DOUBLE CROCHET**
>   **(abbreviated FPdc)**
> YO, insert hook from **front** to **back** around post of st indicated, YO and pull up a loop **even** with loop on hook **(Fig. 11, page 123)**, (YO and draw through 2 loops on hook) twice. Skip sc behind FPdc.

BOBBINS

Wind Red onto 2 bobbins. Work each Red stripe with a separate bobbin and work each Tan section on opposite side of diamond with separate balls of yarn. Always keep unused yarn on the **wrong** side of the Panel.

PANEL (Make 4)

With Tan, ch 50 **loosely**.
Row 1 (Right side): Sc in second ch from hook and in each ch across: 49 sc.
Note: Loop a short piece of yarn around any stitch to mark Row 1 as **right** side and bottom edge.
Row 2: Ch 1, turn; sc in each sc across.
Row 3: Ch 1, turn; sc in first sc, work FPdc around sc in row **below** next sc, sc in next 12 sc changing to Red in last sc worked **(Fig. 22a, page 125)**, sc in next sc changing to Tan, sc in next 9 sc changing to Blue in last sc worked, sc in next sc changing to second ball of Tan, sc in next 9 sc changing to second Red bobbin in last sc worked, sc in next sc changing to Tan, sc in next 12 sc, work FPdc around sc in row **below** next sc, sc in last sc.
Row 4: Ch 1, turn; sc in each st across following Chart, page 109.
Row 5: Ch 1, turn; sc in first sc, work FPdc around FPdc in row **below** next sc, following Chart, sc in each sc across to last 2 sc, work FPdc around FPdc in row **below** next sc, sc in last sc.
Rows 6-284: Repeating Rows 4 and 5, follow Chart Rows 6-42 once, then follow Chart Rows 3-42, 6 times, then follow Chart Rows 3 and 4 once **more**.
Row 285: Ch 1, turn; sc in first sc, work FPdc around FPdc in row **below** next sc, sc in each sc across to last 2 sc, work FPdc around FPdc in row **below** next sc, sc in last sc.
Row 286: Ch 1, turn; sc in each st across; finish off.

ASSEMBLY

Place two Panels with **wrong** sides together and bottom edges at the same end. With Tan, whipstitch Panels together **(Fig. 26b, page 126)**, matching rows, and working through 2 loops at end of rows.
Repeat for remaining Panels, always working from the same direction.

Holding 8 strands of Tan together, add 5" fringe evenly across short edges of Afghan **(Figs. 27a & b, page 126)**.

YOU ARE MY SUNSHINE

*Big, bold sunflowers —
especially ones that never
fade —will brighten anyone's
day. With one look at the
cheery motifs, friends can't
help but smile!*

SUNNY SUNFLOWERS

Finished Size: 52" x 67"

MATERIALS
Worsted Weight Yarn:
Dk Green - 19½ ounces, (550 grams, 1,335 yards)
Yellow - 16½ ounces, (470 grams, 1,130 yards)
Green - 14½ ounces, (410 grams, 995 yards)
Brown - 6½ ounces, (180 grams, 445 yards)
Crochet hook, size I (5.50 mm) **or** size needed for gauge
Yarn needle

GAUGE: Each Square = 7¼"

STITCH GUIDE

CLUSTER (uses one st or sp)
★ YO twice, insert hook in st or sp indicated, YO and pull up a loop, (YO and draw through 2 loops on hook) twice; repeat from ★ once **more**, YO and draw through all 3 loops on hook (***Figs. 16a & b, page 124***).

SQUARE A (Make 32)
With Brown, ch 4; join with slip st to form a ring.
Rnd 1 (Right side): Ch 1, 8 sc in ring; join with slip st to first sc.
Note: Loop a short piece of yarn around any stitch to mark Rnd 1 as **right** side.

Rnd 2: Ch 1, ★ † YO, insert hook in same st, YO and pull up a loop, YO and draw through 1 loop on hook, YO and draw through all 3 loops on hook †, sc in next st; repeat from ★ around, then repeat from † to † once, sc in same st as first st; join with slip st to first st, finish off: 8 sc.
Rnd 3: With **right** side facing, join Yellow with slip st in any sc; ch 3, (tr, ch 1, work Cluster) in same st, ch 1, skip next st, ★ (work Cluster, ch 1) twice in next sc, skip next st; repeat from ★ around; join with slip st to first tr: 16 ch-1 sps.
Rnd 4: Slip st in first ch-1 sp, ch 3, (tr, ch 1, work Cluster) in same sp, ch 1, (work Cluster, ch 1) twice in each ch-1 sp around; join with slip st to first tr, finish off: 32 sts and 32 ch-1 sps.
Rnd 5: With **right** side facing, join Dk Green with slip st in first tr; ch 1, sc in same st, ch 5, sc in next Cluster, ch 4, sc in next Cluster, (ch 3, sc in next Cluster) 5 times, ch 4, ★ sc in next Cluster, ch 5, sc in next Cluster, ch 4, sc in next Cluster, (ch 3, sc in next Cluster) 5 times, ch 4; repeat from ★ around; join with slip st to first sc, finish off: 32 sps.
Rnd 6: With **right** side facing, join Green with slip st in first ch-5 sp; ch 7, tr in same sp (corner made), 3 dc in next ch-4 sp, 3 hdc in next ch-3 sp, 3 sc in next ch-3 sp, sc in next ch-3 sp, 3 sc in next ch-3 sp, 3 hdc in next ch-3 sp, 3 dc in next ch-4 sp, ★ (tr, ch 3, tr) in next ch-5 sp (corner made), 3 dc in next ch-4 sp, 3 hdc in next ch-3 sp, 3 sc in next ch-3 sp, sc in next ch-3 sp, 3 sc in next ch-3 sp, 3 hdc in next ch-3 sp, 3 dc in next ch-4 sp; repeat from ★ around; join with slip st to fourth ch of beginning ch-7, finish off: 84 sts and 4 ch-3 sps.
Rnd 7: With **right** side facing, join Dk Green with slip st in any corner ch-3 sp; ch 3 **(counts as first dc)**, (dc, ch 3, 2 dc) in same sp, dc in each st across to next corner ch-3 sp, ★ (2 dc, ch 3, 2 dc) in corner ch-3 sp, dc in each st across to next corner ch-3 sp; repeat from ★ around; join with slip st to first dc, finish off: 100 dc and 4 ch-3 sps.

SQUARE B (Make 31)
Work same as Square A through Rnd 2; do **not** finish off: 8 sc.
Rnd 3: Ch 3, (tr, ch 1, work Cluster) in same st, ch 1, skip next st, ★ (work Cluster, ch 1) twice in next sc, skip next st; repeat from ★ around; join with slip st to first tr, finish off: 16 ch-1 sps.
Rnd 4: With **right** side facing, join Yellow with slip st in first ch-1 sp; ch 3, (tr, ch 1, work Cluster) in same sp, ch 1, (work Cluster, ch 1) twice in each ch-1 sp around; join with slip st to first tr, finish off: 32 sts and 32 ch-1 sps.
Rnd 5: With Green, repeat Rnd 5 of Square A.
Rnd 6: With Dk Green, repeat Rnd 6 of Square A.
Rnd 7: With Green, repeat Rnd 7 of Square A.

Instructions continued on page 109.

WINTER WARMER

Smaller than most afghans, a cozy lap robe is just the right size for sitting to read or watch television. A friend who enjoys extra warmth will appreciate such a thoughtful gift.

COZY LAP ROBE

Finished Size: 34" x 39"

MATERIALS
  Worsted Weight Yarn:
    Green - 12 ounces, (340 grams, 770 yards)
    Rust - 11 ounces, (310 grams, 705 yards)
  Crochet hook, size I (5.50 mm) **or** size needed for gauge

GAUGE: In pattern, 14 sc and 14 rows = 4"

Gauge Swatch: 5"w x 4"h
Ch 18 **loosely**.
Work same as Afghan Body for 14 rows.
Finish off.

STITCH GUIDE

LEAF
Working **below** next sc, insert hook in sc one row **below** and 2 sc to the **right**, YO and pull up a loop *(Fig. 1a)*, insert hook in sc 2 rows **below** and one sc to the **right**, YO and pull up a loop, insert hook in sc 3 rows **below**, YO and pull up a loop, insert hook in sc 2 rows **below** and one sc to the **left**, YO and pull up a loop, insert hook in sc one row **below** and 2 sc to the **left**, YO and pull up a loop, YO and draw through all 6 loops on hook *(Fig. 1b)*. Skip sc behind Leaf.

Fig. 1a

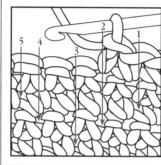

Fig. 1b

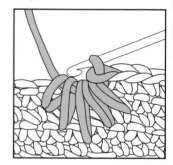

AFGHAN BODY

With Rust, ch 114 **loosely**.
Row 1 (Right side)**:** Sc in second ch from hook and in each ch across: 113 sc.
Note: Loop a short piece of yarn around any stitch to mark Row 1 as **right** side.
Rows 2-4: Ch 1, turn; sc in each sc across changing to Green in last sc worked on Row 4 *(Fig. 22a, page 125)*.
Row 5: Ch 1, turn; sc in first 4 sc, work Leaf, (sc in next 7 sc, work Leaf) across to last 4 sc, sc in last 4 sc: 14 Leaves.
Rows 6-8: Ch 1, turn; sc in each st across changing to Rust in last sc worked on Row 8.
Row 9: Ch 1, turn; sc in first 8 sc, work Leaf, (sc in next 7 sc, work Leaf) across to last 8 sc, sc in last 8 sc: 13 Leaves.
Rows 10-132: Repeat Rows 2-9, 15 times; then repeat Rows 2-4 once **more**; do **not** finish off.

EDGING

Rnd 1: Ch 1, turn; 3 sc in first sc, sc in next 3 sc, work Leaf, (sc in next 7 sc, work Leaf) across to last 4 sc, sc in next 3 sc, 3 sc in last sc; sc in end of each row across; working in free loops of beginning ch *(Fig. 21b, page 125)*, 3 sc in first ch, sc in each ch across to last ch, 3 sc in last ch; sc in end of each row across; join with slip st to first sc.
Rnd 2: Ch 1, do **not** turn; sc in same st, ch 1, sc in top of sc just worked *(Fig. 25, page 126)*, skip next st, (sc in next st, ch 1, sc in top of sc just worked, skip next st) around; join with slip st to first sc, finish off.

YOU'RE AN ANGEL

*Say "thank you" to
a friend who's gone the
extra mile. The filet crochet
cherubs on this lacy afghan
are a lovely way to express
your sentiments.*

CHERUB FILET

Finished Size: 46" x 64"

MATERIALS
Worsted Weight Yarn:
    40 ounces, (1,140 grams, 2,335 yards)
Crochet hook, size G (4.00 mm) **or** size needed
    for gauge

GAUGE: 15 dc and 8 rows = 4"

Gauge Swatch: 4" square
Ch 17 **loosely**.
Row 1: Dc in fourth ch from hook **(3 skipped chs count
as first dc)** and in each ch across: 15 dc.
Rows 2-8: Ch 3 **(counts as first dc)**, turn; dc in next dc
and in each dc across.
Finish off.

STITCH GUIDE

BEGINNING SPACE OVER SPACE
Ch 4, turn; dc in next dc.
BLOCK OVER BLOCK
Dc in next 2 dc.
BLOCK OVER SPACE
Dc in next ch-1 sp, dc in next dc.
SPACE OVER BLOCK
Ch 1, skip next dc, dc in next dc.
SPACE OVER SPACE
Ch 1, dc in next dc.
REVERSE SINGLE CROCHET
    (abbreviated reverse sc)
Working from **left** to **right**, insert hook in st to right of
hook, YO and draw through, under, and to left of loop
on hook (2 loops on hook), YO and draw through both
loops on hook **(Figs. 19a-d, page 125)**.

AFGHAN BODY

Ch 170 **loosely**, place marker in fourth ch from hook for
st placement.
Row 1 (Right side)**:** Dc in sixth ch from hook, ★ ch 1,
skip next ch, dc in next ch; repeat from ★ across: 83 sps.
Row 2: Ch 4 **(counts as first dc plus ch 1, now and
throughout)**, turn; dc in next dc and in each ch-1 sp and
each dc across to last sp, ch 1, skip next ch, dc in next ch:
165 dc and 2 ch-1 sps.
Rows 3-125: Follow Chart, page 108; do **not** finish off.

EDGING

Rnd 1: Ch 3 **(counts as first dc)**, do **not** turn; 2 dc in end
of each row across; working in free loops **(Fig. 21b,
page 125)** and in sps across beginning ch, 3 dc in first
ch, dc in each sp and in each ch across to last sp, dc in last
sp, 3 dc in marked ch, remove marker; 2 dc in end of each
row across; working in sts and in sps on Row 125, 3 dc in
first dc, dc in each sp and in each dc across to last dc, 2 dc
in last dc; join with slip st to first dc.
Rnd 2: Ch 1, work reverse sc in each dc around working
2 reverse sc in center dc of each corner 3-dc group;
join with slip st to first st, finish off.

IT'S YOUR BIRTHDAY!

Stitch up warm wishes for the birthday boy with a thick rainbow-striped throw. The bright "racing" stripes delighted my son, Nicholas – a young man who's always on the go!

RACING STRIPES

Finished Size of Body: 42¹/₂" x 64¹/₂"
Finished Size with Stripes: 45" x 69"

MATERIALS

Worsted Weight Yarn:
Black - 34 ounces, (970 grams, 1,925 yards)
Red - 10¹/₂ ounces, (300 grams, 595 yards)
Orange - 10¹/₂ ounces, (300 grams, 595 yards)
Yellow - 10¹/₂ ounces, (300 grams, 595 yards)
Green - 10¹/₂ ounces, (300 grams, 595 yards)
Blue - 10¹/₂ ounces, (300 grams, 595 yards)
Purple - 10¹/₂ ounces, (300 grams, 595 yards)
Crochet hooks, sizes H (5.00 mm) **and** J (6.00 mm) **or** sizes needed for gauge

GAUGE: With smaller size hook, 13 dc = 4";
6 rows = 3³/₄"

Gauge Swatch: 4"w x 3³/₄"h
With Black, ch 15 **loosely**.
Work same as Afghan Body for 6 rows.
Finish off.

Note #1: This design is reversible. Choose the side you like best as the right side.

Note #2: Each row is worked across length of Afghan.

AFGHAN BODY

With small size hook and Black, ch 212 **loosely**.
Row 1: Dc in fourth ch from hook (**3 skipped chs count as first dc**) and in each ch across: 210 dc.
Rows 2-68: Ch 3 (**counts as first dc**), turn; dc in next dc and in each dc across.
Finish off.

STRIPES

COLOR SEQUENCE

One row **each**: ★ Red, Orange, Yellow, Green, Blue, Purple; repeat from ★ 10 times **more**.

Note: When joining yarn and finishing off, always leave a 9" end to be worked into fringe.

FIRST STRIPE

With **right** side facing and large size hook, join Red with slip st around post of second dc on Row 2; ch 1, 2 sc around same post, (ch 1, 2 sc around post of next dc) across to last dc, leave last dc unworked; finish off.

SECOND STRIPE

With **right** side facing and large size hook, join next color with slip st around post of second dc on next row at **opposite** end from last joining; ch 1, 2 sc around same post, (ch 1, 2 sc around post of next dc) across to last dc, leave last dc unworked; finish off.

REMAINING STRIPES

Work same as Second Stripe working on next 64 rows; leave Row 68 unworked.

Holding 3 strands of corresponding color together, add additional 9" fringe to ends of each Stripe row on Afghan **(Figs. 27a & b, page 126)**.
Holding 4 strands of Purple together, add 9" fringe to each end of Row 1. Holding 4 strands of Red together, add 9" fringe to each end of Row 68.

WEDDING

*The interlocking rings
on this quilt-style
comforter symbolize
the unity of marriage.
What better wedding gift
for a special couple!*

DOUBLE WEDDING RING

Finished Size: 53" x 68"

MATERIALS
  Worsted Weight Yarn:
    Ecru - 26 ounces, (740 gram, 1,785 yards)
    Purple - 15 ounces, (430 grams, 1,030 yards)
    Pink - 15 ounces, (430 grams, 1,030 yards)
    Green - 6 ounces, (170 grams, 410 yards)
  Crochet hook, size G (4.00 mm) **or** size needed
    for gauge
  Yarn needle

GAUGE: Each Square = 2½"
            Each Diamond = 6" in diameter
            Each Oval = 6½" from point to point

Gauge Swatch:
Square: Rnds 1-3 = 2½" square
Diamond: Rnds 1-3 = 2" square
Oval: Rnds 1-5 of Center = 7"w x 3¼"h

SQUARE (Make 32 Purple and 30 Pink)
Ch 4; join with slip st to form a ring.
Rnd 1 (Right side): Ch 1, 12 sc in ring; join with slip st to Back Loop Only of first sc *(Fig. 20, page 125)*.
Note: Loop a short piece of yarn around any stitch to mark Rnd 1 as **right** side.
Rnd 2: Ch 1, turn; (sc, dc) in Front Loop Only of each sc around; join with slip st to Front Loop Only of first sc: 24 sts.
Rnd 3: Ch 3, turn; working in Back Loops Only, (2 dc, ch 1, 2 dc) in next dc, ★ dc in next 5 sts, (2 dc, ch 1, 2 dc) in next dc; repeat from ★ 2 times **more**, dc in last 4 sts; join with slip st to top of beginning ch-3, finish off.

DIAMOND (Make 12)
Note: Diamonds have a tendency to curl until Afghan is assembled.
With Ecru, ch 4; join with slip st to form a ring.
Rnds 1 and 2: Work same as Square: 24 sts.
Rnd 3: Turn; working in Back Loops Only, slip st in next dc, ch 2, (dc, ch 1, dc, hdc) in same st, sc in next 5 sts, ★ (hdc, dc, ch 1, dc, hdc) in next dc, sc in next 5 sts; repeat from ★ 2 times **more**; join with slip st to top of beginning ch-2: 36 sts and 4 ch-1 sps.
Rnd 4: Do **not** turn; working in both loops, slip st in first dc and in next ch-1 sp, ch 2, (dc, ch 1, dc, hdc) in same sp, sc in next 9 sts, ★ (hdc, dc, ch 1, dc, hdc) in next ch-1 sp, sc in next 9 sts; repeat from ★ 2 times **more**; join with slip st to top of beginning ch-2: 52 sts and 4 ch-1 sps.
Rnd 5: Ch 1, turn; working in Front Loops Only, sc in same st, dc in next sc, (sc in next st, dc in next st) 5 times, (sc, dc, sc) in next ch-1 sp, ★ dc in next dc, (sc in next st, dc in next st) 6 times, (sc, dc, sc) in next ch-1 sp; repeat from ★ 2 times **more**, dc in last dc; join with slip st to Front Loop Only of first sc: 64 sts.
Rnd 6: Ch 1, turn; working in Back Loops Only, sc in next 2 sts, (2 sc, ch 3, 2 sc) in next corner dc, ★ sc in next 15 sts, (2 sc, ch 3, 2 sc) in next corner dc; repeat from ★ 2 times **more**, sc in last 13 sts; join with slip st to Back Loop Only of first sc: 76 sc and 4 ch-3 sps.
Rnd 7: Ch 1, turn; working in Front Loops Only, sc in next 15 sc and in next ch, (2 sc, ch 3, 2 sc) in next ch, sc in next ch, ★ sc in next 19 sc and in next ch, (2 sc, ch 3, 2 sc) in next ch, sc in next ch; repeat from ★ 2 times **more**, sc in last 4 sts; join with slip st to **both** loops of first sc; do **not** finish off: 100 sc and 4 ch-3 sps.

Instructions continued on page 109.

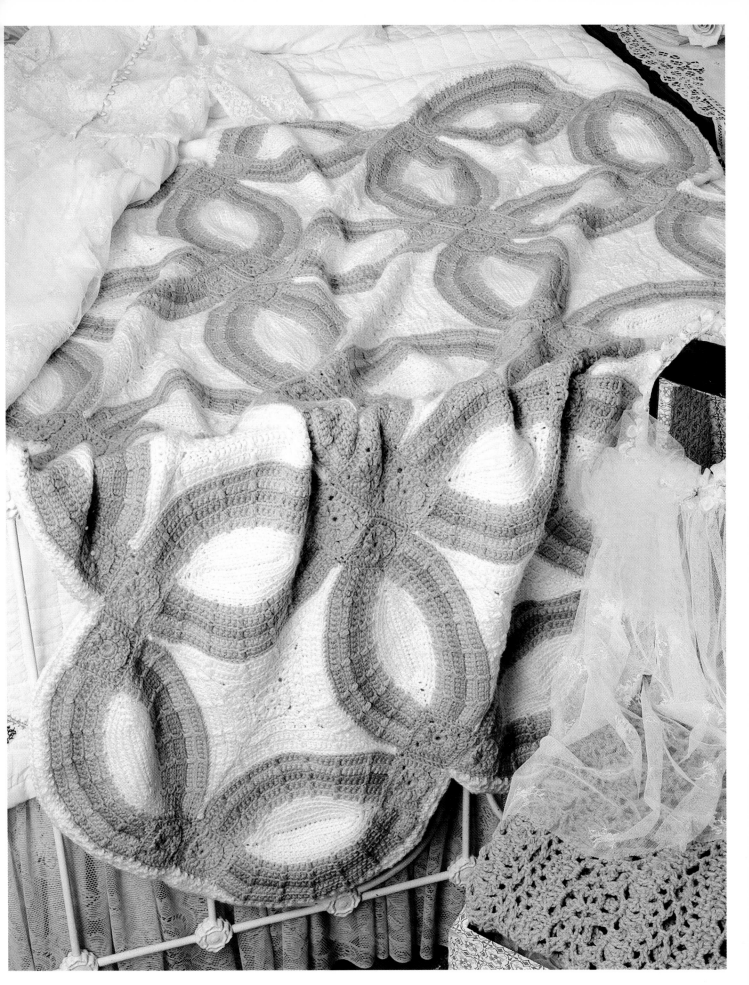

HEARTFELT THANK-YOU

When words aren't enough to express your gratitude to someone who's supported you through good times and bad, this softly colored afghan sends your heartfelt thanks.

TENDER EMBRACE

Finished Size: 53" x 64"

MATERIALS
Worsted Weight Yarn:
Ecru - 31 ounces, (880 grams, 2,125 yards)
Green - 31 ounces, (880 grams, 2,125 yards)
Crochet hook, size H (5.00 mm) **or** size needed for gauge

GAUGE: In pattern, (sc, ch 2) 7 times = 5";
14 rows = 4"

Gauge Swatch: 12½"w x 6"h
Ch 53 **loosely.**
Work same as Afghan Body for 21 rows.

Note: Each row is worked across length of Afghan. When joining yarn and finishing off, always leave a 9" end to be worked into fringe.

STITCH GUIDE

CLUSTER
Ch 3, YO, insert hook in third ch from hook, YO and pull up a loop, YO and draw through 2 loops on hook, YO, insert hook in same ch, YO and pull up a loop, YO and draw through 2 loops on hook, YO and draw through all 3 loops on hook (*Figs. 16a & b, page 124*).

AFGHAN BODY

With Ecru, ch 269 **loosely.**

Row 1 (Right side): Sc in second ch from hook, ★ ch 2, skip next 2 chs, sc in next ch; repeat from ★ across; finish off: 90 sc.

Note: Loop a short piece of yarn around any stitch to mark Row 1 as **right** side.

Row 2: With **wrong** side facing, join Ecru with sc in first sc (*see Joining With Sc, page 125*); (work Cluster, sc in next sc) across; finish off: 90 sc and 89 Clusters.

Row 3: With **right** side facing, join Ecru with sc in first sc; working **behind** Clusters, (ch 2, sc in next sc) across; finish off: 90 sc.

Row 4: With **wrong** side facing, join Green with sc in first sc; (ch 2, sc in next sc) across; finish off.

Row 5: With **right** side facing, join Ecru with sc in first sc; (ch 2, sc in next sc) across; finish off.

Row 6: With **wrong** side facing, join Green with sc in first sc; (ch 2, sc in next sc) twice, (work Cluster, sc in next sc) twice, ★ (ch 2, sc in next sc) 7 times, (work Cluster, sc in next sc) twice; repeat from ★ across to last 4 sc, (ch 2, sc in next sc) 4 times; finish off: 90 sc and 20 Clusters.

Row 7: With **right** side facing, join Ecru with sc in first sc; working **behind** Clusters, (ch 2, sc in next sc) across; finish off.

Row 8: With **wrong** side facing, join Green with sc in first sc; ch 2, sc in next sc, (work Cluster, sc in next sc) 4 times, ★ (ch 2, sc in next sc) 5 times, (work Cluster, sc in next sc) 4 times; repeat from ★ across to last 3 sc, (ch 2, sc in next sc) 3 times; finish off: 90 sc and 40 Clusters.

Row 9: With **right** side facing, join Ecru with sc in first sc; working **behind** Clusters, (ch 2, sc in next sc) across; finish off.

Row 10: With **wrong** side facing, join Green with sc in first sc; ch 2, sc in next sc, (work Cluster, sc in next sc) 5 times, ★ (ch 2, sc in next sc) 4 times, (work Cluster, sc in next sc) 5 times; repeat from ★ across to last 2 sc, (ch 2, sc in next sc) twice; finish off: 90 sc and 50 Clusters.

Row 11: With **right** side facing, join Ecru with sc in first sc; working **behind** Clusters, (ch 2, sc in next sc) across; finish off.

Row 12: With **wrong** side facing, join Green with sc in first sc; (ch 2, sc in next sc) twice, (work Cluster, sc in next sc) 5 times, ★ (ch 2, sc in next sc) 4 times, (work Cluster, sc in next sc) 5 times; repeat from ★ across to last sc, ch 2, sc in last sc; finish off: 90 sc and 50 Clusters.

Rows 13 and 14: Repeat Rows 9 and 10.

Rows 15-17: Repeat Rows 7-9.

Row 18: Repeat Row 6.

Rows 19-21: Repeat Rows 3-5.

Rows 22-183: Repeat Rows 2-21, 8 times; then repeat Rows 2 and 3 once **more.**

Instructions continued on page 111.

A HOMEMADE FRIEND

Teddy bear fans know that a homemade friend lasts longer than one you buy at the store. A good friend will treasure this cuddly pal and rippled afghan to match.

CUDDLY RIPPLE

Finished Size: 46" x 63"

MATERIALS
Worsted Weight Yarn:
    Brown - 15 ounces, (430 grams, 850 yards)
    White - 12 ounces, (340 grams, 680 yards)
    Beige - 6½ ounces, (180 grams, 370 yards)
    Blue - 6 ounces, (170 grams, 340 yards)
Crochet hook, size I (5.50 mm) **or** size needed
    for gauge

GAUGE: Each repeat from point to point and
       5 rows = 4½"

Gauge Swatch: 9"w x 4½"h
Ch 60 **loosely.**
Work same as Afghan Body for 5 rows.

STITCH GUIDE

V-STITCH (*abbreviated V-St*)
(Dc, ch 1, dc) in st or sp indicated.
DECREASE (uses next 2 ch-1 sps)
YO, insert hook in next ch-1 sp, YO and pull up a loop,
YO and draw through 2 loops on hook, YO, skip next
3 dc, insert hook in next ch-1 sp, YO and pull up a loop,
YO and draw through 2 loops on hook, YO and draw
through all 3 loops on hook (**counts as one dc**).

ENDING DECREASE
(uses next ch-1 sp and last 3 dc)
YO, insert hook in next ch-1 sp, YO and pull up a loop,
YO and draw through 2 loops on hook, YO, skip next
2 dc, insert hook in last dc, YO and pull up a loop,
YO and draw through 2 loops on hook, YO and draw
through all 3 loops on hook (**counts as one dc**).

AFGHAN BODY
With Brown, ch 284 **loosely.**
Row 1 (Right side)**:** Dc in fifth ch from hook (**4 skipped chs count as first dc plus one skipped ch**), (skip next 2 chs, work V-St in next ch) 4 times, ch 3, work V-St in next ch, (skip next 2 chs, work V-St in next ch) 3 times, ★ [(YO, skip next 2 chs, insert hook in next ch, YO and pull up a loop, YO and draw through 2 loops on hook) twice, YO and draw through all 3 loops on hook (**counts as one dc**)], (skip next 2 chs, work V-St in next ch) 4 times, ch 3, work V-St in next ch, (skip next 2 chs, work V-St in next ch) 3 times; repeat from ★ across to last 5 chs, [YO, skip next 2 chs, insert hook in next ch, YO and pull up a loop, YO and draw through 2 loops on hook, YO, skip next ch, insert hook in last ch, YO and pull up a loop, YO and draw through 2 loops on hook, YO and draw through all 3 loops on hook (**counts as one dc**)]; finish off: 80 V-Sts and 10 ch-3 sps.
Note: Loop a short piece of yarn around any stitch to mark Row 1 as **right** side.
Row 2: With **wrong** side facing, join Beige with slip st in first dc; ch 3 (**counts as first dc, now and throughout**), dc in next V-St (ch-1 sp), work V-St in next 3 V-Sts, work (V-St, ch 3, V-St) in next ch-3 sp, work V-St in next 3 V-Sts, ★ decrease, work V-St in next 3 V-Sts, work (V-St, ch 3, V-St) in next ch-3 sp, work V-St in next 3 V-Sts; repeat from ★ across to last V-St, work ending decrease; finish off.
Row 3: With **right** side facing, join Brown with slip st in first dc; ch 3, dc in next V-St, work V-St in next 3 V-Sts, work (V-St, ch 3, V-St) in next ch-3 sp, work V-St in next 3 V-Sts, ★ decrease, work V-St in next 3 V-Sts, work (V-St, ch 3, V-St) in next ch-3 sp, work V-St in next 3 V-Sts; repeat from ★ across to last V-St, work ending decrease; finish off.
Row 4: With White, repeat Row 2.
Row 5: With Blue, repeat Row 3.
Row 6: With White, repeat Row 2.
Row 7: Repeat Row 3.
Rows 8-69: Repeat Rows 2-7, 10 times; then repeat Rows 2 and 3 once **more**; at end of Row 69, do **not** finish off.

Instructions continued on page 58.

EDGING

With Brown, ch 2, do **not** turn; dc in top of last dc made on Row 69; working in end of rows, skip first row, (slip st, ch 2, dc) in top of each row across; working in free loops (*Fig. 21b, page 125*) and in sps of beginning ch, slip st in first ch, (ch 3, slip st in next ch-2 sp) 4 times, slip st in next 2 chs (at base of next 2 V-Sts), (slip st in next ch-2 sp, ch 3) 4 times, ★ (slip st, ch 3, slip st) in next ch-2 sp, (ch 3, slip st in next ch-2 sp) 4 times, slip st in next 2 chs (at base of next 2 V-Sts), (slip st in next ch-2 sp, ch 3) 4 times; repeat from ★ 8 times **more**, skip ch at base of next dc and next ch, (slip st, ch 2, dc) in next ch; working in end of rows, (slip st, ch 2, dc) in top of each row across to last row, skip last row; working in sts on Row 69, skip first dc, slip st in next dc, ch 3, (slip st in next V-St, ch 3) 4 times, (slip st, ch 3, slip st) in next ch-3 sp, (ch 3, slip st in next V-St) 4 times, † skip next dc, slip st in next 2 dc and in next ch-1 sp, ch 3, (slip st in next V-St, ch 3) 3 times, (slip st, ch 3, slip st) in next ch-3 sp, (ch 3, slip st in next V-St) 4 times †, repeat from † to † across to last 2 dc, ch 3, skip last 2 dc; join with slip st at base of beginning ch-2, finish off.

TEDDY BEAR

Finished Size: 20" tall

MATERIALS
Worsted Weight Yarn:
  Brown - 7½ ounces, (220 grams, 425 yards)
  Black - small amount for nose and mouth
Crochet hook, size H (5.00 mm) **or** size needed
  for gauge
Polyester fiberfill
Yarn needle
Sewing needle and thread
¾" Buttons - 4
1½"w Ribbon - 1¼" yards

GAUGE: In pattern, 2 dc, (FPdc, 2 dc) 3 times = 3½";
      6 rows = 3¼"

Gauge Swatch: 3½" diameter
Work same as Muzzle and Head through Rnd 3.

STITCH GUIDE

> **FRONT POST DOUBLE CROCHET**
>   (*abbreviated FPdc*)
> YO, insert hook from **front** to **back** around post of st indicated, YO and pull up a loop (*Fig. 11, page 123*), (YO and draw through 2 loops on hook) twice.
> **DECREASE** (uses next 2 dc)
> ★ YO, insert hook in **next** dc, YO and pull up a loop, YO and draw through 2 loops on hook; repeat from ★ once **more**, YO and draw through all 3 loops on hook (**counts as one dc**).

MUZZLE AND HEAD

With Brown, ch 4; join with slip st to form a ring.
Rnd 1 (Right side): Ch 3 (**counts as first dc, now and throughout**), 11 dc in ring; join with slip st to first dc: 12 dc.
Rnd 2: Ch 3, dc in same st, work FPdc around next dc, skip dc behind FPdc, ★ 2 dc in next dc, work FPdc around next dc, skip dc behind FPdc; repeat from ★ around; join with slip st to first dc: 18 sts.
Rnd 3: Ch 3, 2 dc in next dc, work FPdc around next FPdc, ★ dc in next dc, 2 dc in next dc, work FPdc around next FPdc; repeat from ★ around; join with slip st to first dc: 24 sts.
Rnd 4: Ch 1, sc in same st and in next 2 dc, skip next FPdc, (sc in next 3 dc, skip next FPdc) around; join with slip st to first sc: 18 sc.
Rnd 5: Ch 3, 3 dc in next sc, dc in next sc, work FPdc around next FPdc on Rnd 3, ★ dc in next sc on Rnd 4, 3 dc in next sc, dc in next sc, work FPdc around next FPdc on Rnd 3; repeat from ★ around; join with slip st to first dc: 36 sts.
Rnd 6: Ch 3, dc in next dc, work FPdc around next dc, skip dc behind FPdc, dc in next 2 dc, work FPdc around next FPdc, ★ dc in next 2 dc, work FPdc around next dc, skip dc behind FPdc, dc in next 2 dc, work FPdc around next FPdc; repeat from ★ around; join with slip st to first dc.
Rnd 7: Ch 3, 2 dc in next dc, work FPdc around next FPdc, ★ dc in next dc, 2 dc in next dc, work FPdc around next FPdc; repeat from ★ around; join with slip st to first dc: 48 sts.
Rnds 8-12: Ch 3, dc in next 2 dc, work FPdc around next FPdc, (dc in next 3 dc, work FPdc around next FPdc) around; join with slip st to first dc.
Rnd 13: Ch 3, decrease, work FPdc around next FPdc, ★ dc in next dc, decrease, work FPdc around next FPdc; repeat from ★ around; join with slip st to first dc: 36 sts.

Rnd 14: Ch 2, dc in next dc, work FPdc around next FPdc, (decrease, work FPdc around next FPdc) around; join with slip st to first dc: 24 sts.
Stuff Head and Muzzle lightly with polyester fiberfill.
Rnd 15: Ch 2, work FPdc around next FPdc, ★ YO, insert hook in next dc, YO and pull up a loop, YO and draw through 2 loops on hook, YO, insert hook from **front** to **back** around next FPdc, YO and pull up a loop, YO and draw through 2 loops on hook, YO and draw through all 3 loops on hook; repeat from ★ around; join with slip st to first FPdc, finish off leaving a long end for sewing.
Thread yarn needle with long end and weave through remaining sts on Rnd 15; gather tightly and secure end.

BODY

With Brown, ch 36 **loosely**; being careful not to twist ch, join with slip st to form a ring.
Rnd 1 (Right side): Ch 3, dc in next ch and in each ch around; join with slip st to first dc: 36 dc.
Rnd 2: Ch 3, dc in same st, work FPdc around next dc, skip dc behind FPdc, ★ 2 dc in next dc, work FPdc around next dc, skip dc behind FPdc; repeat from ★ around; join with slip st to first dc: 54 sts.
Rnds 3-12: Ch 3, dc in next dc, work FPdc around next FPdc, (dc in next 2 dc, work FPdc around next FPdc) around; join with slip st to first dc.
Rnd 13: Ch 2, dc in next dc, work FPdc around next FPdc, (decrease, work FPdc around next FPdc) around; join with slip st to first dc: 36 sts.
Rnd 14: Ch 3, work FPdc around next FPdc, (dc in next dc, work FPdc around next FPdc) around; join with slip st to first dc.
Stuff Body lightly with polyester fiberfill.
Rnd 15: Ch 2, work FPdc around next FPdc, ★ YO, insert hook in next dc, YO and pull up a loop, YO and draw through 2 loops on hook, YO, insert hook from **front** to **back** around next FPdc, YO and pull up a loop, YO and draw through 2 loops on hook, YO and draw through all 3 loops on hook; repeat from ★ around; join with slip st to first FPdc: 18 sts.
Rnd 16: Ch 1, ★ (YO, insert hook from **front** to **back** around second leg of **next** st, YO and pull up a loop, YO and draw through 2 loops on hook) twice, YO and draw through all 3 loops on hook; repeat from ★ around; join with slip st to first st, finish off leaving a long end for sewing.
Thread yarn needle with long end and weave through remaining sts on Rnd 16; gather tightly and secure end.

Using photo as a guide for placement, tilt Head with Muzzle forward and horizontal and sew to free loops of beginning ch of Body (*Fig. 21b, page 125*).

ARM (Make 2)

With Brown, ch 4; join with slip st to form a ring.
Rnd 1 (Right side): Ch 3, 11 dc in ring; join with slip st to first dc: 12 dc.
Rnd 2: Ch 3, dc in same st, work FPdc around next dc, skip dc behind FPdc, ★ 2 dc in next dc, work FPdc around next dc, skip dc behind FPdc; repeat from ★ around; join with slip st to first dc: 18 sts.
Rnds 3-13: Ch 3, dc in next dc, work FPdc around next FPdc, (dc in next 2 dc, work FPdc around next FPdc) around; join with slip st to first dc.
Stuff Arm lightly with polyester fiberfill.
Rnd 14: Ch 2, dc in next dc, work FPdc around next FPdc, (decrease, work FPdc around next FPdc) around; join with slip st to first dc, finish off leaving a long end for sewing.
Thread yarn needle with long end and weave through remaining sts on Rnd 14; gather tightly and secure end.
Form elbow by tacking Rnds 5 and 9 together at center of rnd between 2 FPdc.

LEG (Make 2)

With Brown, ch 8 **loosely**.
Rnd 1 (Right side): 2 Sc in second ch from hook, sc in next 5 chs, 3 sc in last ch; working in free loops of beginning ch, sc in next 6 chs; join with slip st to first sc: 16 sc.
Rnd 2: Ch 1, 2 sc in same st and in next sc, sc in next 5 sc, 2 sc in each of next 3 sc, sc in next 5 sc, 2 sc in last sc; join with slip st to first sc: 22 sc.
Rnd 3: Ch 1, 2 sc in same st and in each of next 2 sc, sc in next 7 sc, 2 sc in each of next 4 sc, sc in next 7 sc, 2 sc in last sc; join with slip st to first sc: 30 sc.
Rnd 4: Ch 3, dc in next sc and in each sc around; join with slip st to first dc.
Rnd 5: Ch 3, dc in next dc, work FPdc around next dc, skip dc behind FPdc, ★ dc in next 2 dc, work FPdc around next dc, skip dc behind FPdc; repeat from ★ around; join with slip st to first dc.
Rnd 6: Ch 3, dc in next dc, work FPdc around next FPdc, (dc in next 2 dc, work FPdc around next FPdc) 3 times, (decrease, work FPdc around next FPdc) 4 times, (dc in next 2 dc, work FPdc around next FPdc) twice; join with slip st to first dc: 26 sts.
Rnd 7: Ch 3, dc in next dc, work FPdc around next FPdc, (dc in next 2 dc, work FPdc around next FPdc) 3 times, ★ YO, insert hook in next dc, YO and pull up a loop, YO and draw through 2 loops on hook, YO, insert hook from **front** to **back** around next FPdc, YO and pull up a loop, YO and draw through 2 loops on hook, YO and draw through all 3 loops on hook; repeat from ★ 3 times **more**, (dc in next 2 dc, work FPdc around next FPdc) twice; join with slip st to first dc; do **not** finish off: 22 sts.

Instructions continued on page 111.

BIRTHDAY WISHES

*Surprise a dear friend with a
lovely afghan on her birthday.
Mile-a-minute designs like
this one are easy to work into
your schedule when you're
on the go as much as I am.*

SOFT MILE-A-MINUTE

Finished Size: 49" x 69"

MATERIALS
Worsted Weight Yarn:
Pink - 47 ounces, (1,330 grams, 2,740 yards)
Off-White - 24 ounces, (680 grams, 1,400 yards)
Crochet hook, size H (5.00 mm) **or** size needed
for gauge
Yarn needle

GAUGE: 15 dc = 3³/₄"
Each Strip = 3¹/₂" wide

Gauge Swatch: 3¹/₂"w x 11¹/₂"h
Foundation Row (Right side)**:** With Off-White,
(ch 4, work Cluster) 4 times, ch 1; finish off: 4 Clusters.
Rnds 1-3: Work same as Strip.

STITCH GUIDE

CLUSTER
YO, insert hook in third ch from hook, YO and pull up
a loop, YO and draw through 2 loops on hook, YO,
insert hook in same ch, YO and pull up a loop, YO and
draw through 2 loops on hook, YO and draw through all
3 loops on hook (*Figs. 16a & b, page 124*).

Stitch Guide continued on page 111.

STRIP (Make 14)
Foundation Row (Right side)**:** With Off-White, (ch 4,
work Cluster) 50 times, ch 1; finish off: 50 Clusters.
Note: Loop a short piece of yarn around last stitch to mark
right side and top.
Rnd 1: With **right** side facing, join Pink with slip st in last
ch-1 on Foundation Row; ch 3 (**counts as first dc, now
and throughout**), 10 dc in same ch, (skip next Cluster, 5 dc
in ch **before** next Cluster) across to last Cluster, skip last
Cluster, 11 dc in first ch of beginning ch-4; working in free
loops of chs (*Fig. 21b, page 125*), skip first Cluster, (5 dc
in ch **before** next Cluster, skip next Cluster) across; join
with slip st to first dc, finish off: 512 dc.
Rnd 2: With **right** side facing, join Off-White with slip st
in same st as joining; ch 3, dc in next dc, work FPdc around
next dc (*see Stitch Guide, page 111*), (2 dc in each of
next 2 dc, work FPdc around next dc) twice, (dc in next
4 dc, work FPdc around next dc) across to fourth dc of next
11-dc group, place marker around last FPdc made for st
placement, (2 dc in each of next 2 dc, work FPdc around
next dc) twice, (dc in next 4 dc, work FPdc around next
dc) across to last 2 dc, place marker around last FPdc made
for st placement, dc in last 2 dc; join with slip st to first dc,
finish off: 520 sts.
Rnd 3: With **right** side facing, join Pink with slip st in
same st as joining; ch 3, dc in next dc, skip next FPdc, 2 dc
in each of next 2 dc, working in **front** of last 4 dc made,
work Beginning Split tr, working **behind** Beginning Split tr
just made, 2 dc in each of 2 skipped dc and in each of next
2 dc, † working in **front** of last 4 dc made, work Split tr,
working **behind** Split tr just made, 2 dc in each of 2 skipped
dc, dc in next 2 dc, working in **front** of last 2 dc made,
work Split tr, ★ working **behind** Split tr just made, dc in
2 skipped dc and in next 2 dc, working in **front** of last 2 dc
made, work Split tr; repeat from ★ across working last leg
of last Split tr in next marked FPdc, working **behind**
Split tr just made, dc in 2 skipped dc †, 2 dc in each of next
2 dc, working in **front** of last 4 dc made, work Split tr,
working **behind** Split tr just made, 2 dc in each of 2 skipped
dc and in each of next 2 dc, repeat from † to † once, dc in
next 2 dc, working in **front** of last 2 dc made, work Ending
Split tr; join with slip st to first dc, finish off.

ASSEMBLY
Place two Strips together with top edges at the same end.
With Pink and working through both loops, whipstitch two
Strips together (*Fig. 26b, page 126*), beginning in first
Split tr on side and ending in last Split tr on same side.
Join remaining Strips in same manner, always working in
the same direction.

A GOOD FRIEND

A good friend, like an afghan, is comforting, warm, and always appreciated. Share this sentiment with a rich diamond-pattern wrap.

RICH DIAMONDS

Finished Size: 48" x 69"

MATERIALS
Worsted Weight Yarn:
    Blue - 20 ounces, (570 grams, 1,130 yards)
    Maroon - 15 ounces, (430 grams, 850 yards)
    Tan - 13 ounces, (370 grams, 735 yards)
Crochet hook, size H (5.00 mm) **or** size needed
    for gauge
Yarn needle

GAUGE: Each Diamond = 8"w x 11½"h

Gauge Swatch: 3¾"w x 5½"h
Work same as Diamond A through Rnd 2.

STITCH GUIDE

BEGINNING CLUSTER
Ch 3, ★ YO, insert hook in sp indicated, YO and pull up a loop, YO and draw through 2 loops on hook; repeat from ★ once **more**, YO and draw through all 3 loops on hook (*Figs. 16a & b, page 124*).

CLUSTER
★ YO, insert hook in st or sp indicated, YO and pull up a loop, YO and draw through 2 loops on hook; repeat from ★ 2 times **more**, YO and draw through all 4 loops on hook.

DIAMOND A (Make 36)
With Blue, ch 4; join with slip st to form a ring.
Rnd 1 (Right side): Ch 3 (**counts as first dc, now and throughout**), in ring work (2 dc, 2 tr, ch 3, 2 tr, 3 dc, ch 2, 3 dc, 2 tr, ch 3, 2 tr, 3 dc), ch 2; join with slip st to first dc: 20 sts and 4 sps.
Note: Loop a short piece of yarn around any stitch to mark Rnd 1 as **right** side.
Rnd 2: Ch 3, dc in next 4 sts, † (dc, 2 tr, ch 2, 2 tr, dc) in next ch-3 sp, dc in next 5 sts, (dc, ch 2, dc) in next ch-2 sp †, dc in next 5 sts, repeat from † to † once; join with slip st to first dc, finish off: 36 sts and 4 sps.
Rnd 3: With **right** side facing, join Tan with slip st in last ch-2 sp worked, work (Beginning Cluster, ch 2, Cluster) in same sp, † ch 1, (skip next st, work Cluster in next st, ch 1) 4 times, skip next st, work (Cluster, ch 3, Cluster) in next ch-2 sp, ch 1, (skip next st, work Cluster in next st, ch 1) 4 times, skip next st †, work (Cluster, ch 2, Cluster) in next ch-2 sp, repeat from † to † once; join with slip st to top of Beginning Cluster, finish off: 24 Clusters.
Rnd 4: With **right** side facing, join Blue with slip st in first ch-2 sp; ch 3, (dc, ch 2, 2 dc) in same sp, † 2 dc in each of next 5 ch-1 sps, (3 dc, 2 tr, ch 3, 2 tr, 3 dc) in next ch-3 sp, 2 dc in each of next 5 ch-1 sps †, (2 dc, ch 2, 2 dc) in next ch-2 sp, repeat from † to † once; join with slip st to first dc: 68 sts and 4 sps.
Rnd 5: Ch 3, dc in next dc, † (dc, ch 2, dc) in next ch-2 sp, dc in next 17 sts, (2 dc, 2 tr, ch 2, 2 tr, 2 dc) in next ch-3 sp †, dc in next 17 sts, repeat from † to † once, dc in last 15 sts; join with slip st to first dc, finish off: 88 sts and 4 sps.

DIAMOND B (Make 25)
With Maroon in place of Blue, work same as Diamond A.

ASSEMBLY
With matching colors as desired, using Placement Diagram, page 112, as a guide, and working through inside loops only, whipstitch Diamonds together, forming strips (*Fig. 26a, page 126*), beginning in second ch of first corner ch-2 and ending in first ch of next corner ch-2; whipstitch strips together in same manner, securing seam at each corner.

Attach a Blue Tassel in each point across each end of Afghan (*Figs. 28a & b, page 127*).

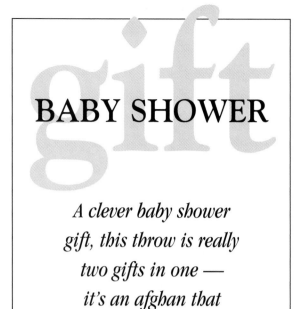

BABY SHOWER

A clever baby shower gift, this throw is really two gifts in one — it's an afghan that folds into itself to make a cushy pillow!

BABY YO-YO PILLOWGHAN

Finished Size: 38" x 50½"

MATERIALS
Worsted Weight Yarn:
 White - 24 ounces, (680 grams, 1,520 yards)
 Pink - 8 ounces, (230 grams, 505 yards)
 Blue - 2 ounces, (60 grams, 125 yards)
 Green - 2 ounces, (60 grams, 125 yards)
 Yellow - 2 ounces, (60 grams, 125 yards)
 Crochet hook, size F (3.75 mm) **or** size needed for gauge

GAUGE: Each Square = 12½"

Gauge Swatch: 2½" square
Work same as First Motif.

PILLOW SQUARE (Make 2)
FIRST MOTIF
With Green, ch 6; join with slip st to form a ring.
Rnd 1 (Right side): Ch 1, (sc in ring, ch 2) 12 times; join with slip st to Back Loop Only *(Fig. 20, page 125)* of first sc changing to White *(Fig. 22b, page 125)*, cut first color: 12 sc and 12 ch-2 sps.
Note: Loop a short piece of yarn around any stitch to mark Rnd 1 as **right** side.

Rnd 2: Ch 1, working in Back Loops Only, sc in same st, ch 3, (sc, ch 5, sc) in next sc, ★ ch 3, (sc in next sc, ch 3) twice, (sc, ch 5, sc) in next sc; repeat from ★ 2 times **more**, ch 3, sc in next sc, ch 3; join with slip st to **both** loops of first sc, finish off: 16 sc and 4 ch-5 sps.

ADDITIONAL MOTIFS
With next color indicated on Motif Placement Diagram, ch 6; join with slip st to form a ring.
Rnd 1: Work same as First Motif: 12 sc and 12 ch-2 sps.
Rnd 2 (Joining rnd): Following Motif Placement Diagram, work One or Two Side Joining.

MOTIF PLACEMENT DIAGRAM

C	A	D	B
D	B	C	A
A	C	B	D
B	D	A	C

KEY
A - Blue
B - Pink
C - Green
D - Yellow

ONE SIDE JOINING
Rnd 2 (Joining rnd): Ch 1, working in Back Loops Only, sc in same st, ch 3, ★ (sc, ch 5, sc) in next sc, ch 3, (sc in next sc, ch 3) twice; repeat from ★ once **more**, sc in next sc, ch 2, holding Motifs with **wrong** sides together, sc in corresponding corner ch-5 sp on **adjacent Motif** *(Fig. 24, page 126)*, ch 2, sc in same sc on **new Motif**, (ch 1, sc in next ch-3 sp on **adjacent Motif**, ch 1, sc in next sc on **new Motif**) 3 times, ch 2, sc in corresponding corner ch-5 sp on **adjacent Motif**, ch 2, sc in same sc on **new Motif**, ch 3, sc in last sc, ch 3; join with slip st to **both** loops of first sc, finish off.

TWO SIDE JOINING
Rnd 2 (Joining rnd): Ch 1, working in Back Loops Only, sc in same st, ch 3, (sc, ch 5, sc) in next sc, ch 3, (sc in next sc, ch 3) twice, sc in next sc, ch 2, holding Motifs with **wrong** sides together, sc in corresponding corner ch-5 sp on **adjacent Motif**, ch 2, sc in same sc on **new Motif**, (ch 1, sc in next ch-3 sp on **adjacent Motif**, ch 1, sc in next sc on **new Motif**) 3 times, ch 2, sc in each of next 3 corner sps on **adjacent Motifs**, ch 2, sc in same sc on **new Motif**, (ch 1, sc in next ch-3 sp on **adjacent Motif**, ch 1, sc in next sc on **new Motif**) 3 times, ch 2, sc in next corner ch-5 sp on **adjacent Motif**, ch 2, sc in same sc on **new Motif**, ch 3, sc in last sc, ch 3; join with slip st to **both** loops of first sc, finish off.

Instructions continued on page 112.

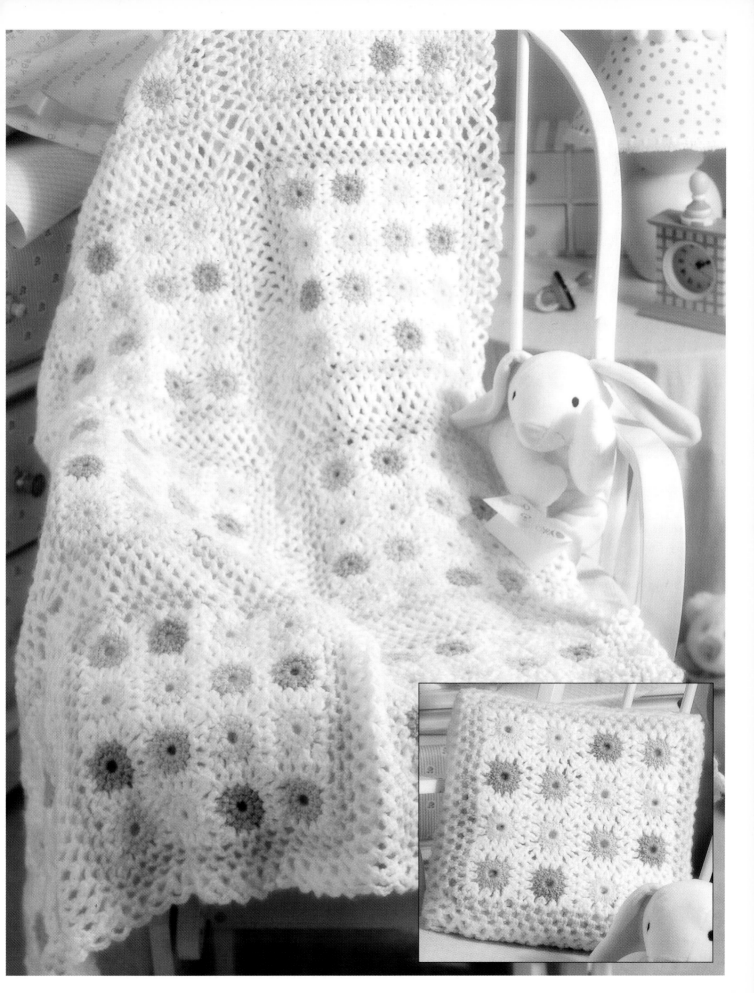

THOUGHTS OF YOU

The dainty fans and lacy edging of this graceful afghan create a wistful Victorian feeling. The wrap is an elegant memento for someone with whom you've shared sentimental moments.

GRACEFUL FANS

Finished Size: 53" x 68"

MATERIALS
Worsted Weight Yarn:
    56 ounces, (1,590 grams, 2,705 yards)
    Crochet hook, size G (4.00 mm) **or** size needed for gauge

GAUGE: In pattern, (9 tr, dc) twice = 4½";
            6 rows = 4"

Gauge Swatch: 6¾"w x 4"h
Ch 34 **loosely.**
Work same as Afghan Body for 6 rows.
Finish off.

STITCH GUIDE

PICOT
Ch 3, slip st in top of tr just made *(Fig. 25, page 126)*.

AFGHAN BODY

Ch 204 **loosely**, place marker in fourth ch from hook for st placement.

Row 1: Dc in sixth ch from hook, ★ ch 1, skip next ch, dc in next ch; repeat from ★ across: 100 dc and 100 sps.

Row 2 (Right side): Ch 4, turn; 4 tr in first dc, skip next 2 ch-1 sps, dc in next ch-1 sp, ★ skip next 2 dc, 9 tr in next dc, skip next 2 ch-1 sps, dc in next ch-1 sp; repeat from ★ across to last 2 dc, skip last 2 dc and next ch, 5 tr in next ch: 180 tr and 20 dc.

Row 3: Ch 3 **(counts as first dc, now and throughout)**, turn; dc in next tr, ch 1, ★ skip next tr, dc in next st, ch 1; repeat from ★ across to last 2 tr, skip next tr, dc in last tr and in next ch: 102 dc and 99 ch-1 sps.

Row 4: Ch 3, turn; skip next 2 dc, 9 tr in next dc, ★ skip next 2 ch-1 sps, dc in next ch-1 sp, skip next 2 dc, 9 tr in next dc; repeat from ★ across to last 3 dc, skip next 2 dc, dc in last dc: 180 tr and 21 dc.

Row 5: Ch 4, turn; skip next tr, dc in next tr, ★ ch 1, skip next tr, dc in next st; repeat from ★ across: 100 dc and 100 sps.

Row 6: Ch 4, turn; 4 tr in first dc, skip next 2 ch-1 sps, dc in next ch-1 sp, ★ skip next 2 dc, 9 tr in next dc, skip next 2 ch-1 sps, dc in next ch-1 sp; repeat from ★ across to last 2 dc, skip last 2 dc and next ch, 5 tr in next ch: 180 tr and 20 dc.

Row 7: Ch 3, turn; dc in next tr, ch 1, ★ skip next tr, dc in next st, ch 1; repeat from ★ across to last 2 tr, skip next tr, dc in last tr and in next ch: 102 dc and 99 ch-1 sps.

Rows 8-91: Repeat Rows 4-7, 21 times; do **not** finish off.

EDGING

Rnd 1: Ch 4 **(counts as first tr)**, turn; 8 tr in same st, ch 2, skip next ch-1 sp, sc in next ch, ch 2, (skip next 2 ch-1 sps, 7 tr in next ch, ch 2, skip next 2 ch-1 sps, sc in next ch, ch 2) across to last 3 dc, skip next 2 dc, 9 tr in last dc, † ch 2; working in end of rows, skip first row, sc in next row, ch 2, (skip next row, 7 tr in next row, ch 2, skip next row, sc in next row, ch 2) across to last row, skip last row †; working in free loops of beginning ch *(Fig. 21b, page 125)*, 9 tr in marked ch, ch 2, skip next 3 chs, sc in next ch, ch 2, ★ skip next 5 chs, 7 tr in next ch, ch 2, skip next 5 chs, sc in next ch, ch 2; repeat from ★ across to last 4 chs, skip next 3 chs, 9 tr in last ch, repeat from † to † once; join with slip st to first tr: 568 tr and 80 sc.

Rnd 2: Ch 5, do **not** turn; tr in next tr, (ch 1, tr in next tr) 7 times, ★ † ch 2, dc in next sc, ch 2, [tr in next tr, (ch 1, tr in next tr) 6 times, ch 2, dc in next sc, ch 2] across to next corner 9-tr group †, tr in next tr, (ch 1, tr in next tr) 8 times; repeat from ★ 2 times **more**, then repeat from † to † once; join with slip st to fourth ch of beginning ch-5; do **not** finish off.

Instructions continued on page 113.

"When this you see, remember me and think of one who thinks of thee."

MY BEST FRIEND

The next time you drop in on your best friend, carry along something that will truly delight her — a handmade gift from you! The genteel pattern and lush fringe will wrap her in good will.

ELEGANT CLUSTERS

Finished Size: 51" x 71"

MATERIALS
Worsted Weight Yarn:
    42 ounces, (1,190 grams, 2,760 yards)
Crochet hook, size I (5.50 mm) **or** size needed
    for gauge

GAUGE: 3 repeats = 6"

Gauge Swatch: 6¼"w x 4¼"h
Ch 26 **loosely**.
Work same as Afghan Body for 11 rows.

STITCH GUIDE

CLUSTER
Ch 3, YO, insert hook in third ch from hook, YO and pull up a loop, YO and draw through 2 loops on hook, YO, insert hook in same ch, YO and pull up a loop, YO and draw through 2 loops on hook, YO and draw through all 3 loops on hook *(Figs. 16a & b, page 124)*.

AFGHAN BODY
Ch 194 **loosely**.

Row 1 (Right side): Sc in second ch from hook and in next ch, ch 3, skip next 2 chs, dc in next ch, ch 3, ★ skip next 2 chs, sc in next 3 chs, ch 3, skip next 2 chs, dc in next ch, ch 3; repeat from ★ across to last 4 chs, skip next 2 chs, sc in last 2 chs: 48 ch-3 sps.

Row 2: Ch 5, turn; sc in next ch-3 sp, work Cluster, sc in next ch-3 sp, ch 2, skip next sc, dc in next st, ★ ch 2, sc in next ch-3 sp, work Cluster, sc in next ch-3 sp, ch 2, skip next sc, dc in next st; repeat from ★ across: 24 Clusters.

Row 3: Ch 6 (**counts as first dc plus ch 3, now and throughout**), turn; sc in next sc, working **behind** next Cluster, dc in dc **below** Cluster, sc in next sc, ch 3, ★ dc in next dc, ch 3, sc in next sc, working **behind** next Cluster, dc in dc **below** Cluster, sc in next sc, ch 3; repeat from ★ across to last ch-5, skip next 2 chs, dc in next ch: 48 sc.

Row 4: Ch 1, turn; sc in first dc and in next ch-3 sp, ch 2, skip next sc, dc in next dc, ch 2, sc in next ch-3 sp, ★ work Cluster, sc in next ch-3 sp, ch 2, skip next sc, dc in next dc, ch 2, sc in next ch-3 sp; repeat from ★ across to last dc, sc in last dc: 23 Clusters.

Row 5: Ch 1, turn; sc in first 2 sc, ch 3, dc in next dc, ch 3, ★ sc in next sc, working **behind** next Cluster, dc in dc **below** Cluster, sc in next sc, ch 3, dc in next dc, ch 3; repeat from ★ across to last 2 sc, sc in last 2 sc: 50 sc.
Repeat Rows 2-5 until Afghan Body measures approximately 68" from beginning ch, ending by working Row 3; do **not** finish off.

EDGING
Rnd 1: Ch 4, do **not** turn; hdc in same dc (corner made), ch 1; working in end of rows, skip first row, (hdc in top of next row, ch 1) twice, [skip next sc row, (hdc in top of next row, ch 1) 3 times] across, (hdc, ch 2, hdc) in ch at base of first sc on Row 1 (corner made), ★ ch 1, (hdc in next ch-2 sp, ch 1) twice, skip ch at base of next sc, hdc in ch at base of next sc; repeat from ★ across, ch 2, hdc in same ch (corner made), ch 1; working in end of rows, hdc in top of first row, (ch 1, hdc in top of next row) twice, [ch 1, skip next sc row, hdc in top of next row, (ch 1, hdc in top of next row) twice] across, ch 2, hdc in same row (corner made), ch 1, hdc in next ch-3 sp, ch 1, skip next sc, hdc in next dc, ch 1, [(hdc in next ch-3 sp, ch 1) twice, skip next sc, hdc in next dc, ch 1] across to last ch-3 sp, hdc in last ch-3 sp, ch 1; join with slip st to second ch of beginning ch-4.

Rnd 2: ★ (Slip st, ch 2) twice in corner ch-2 sp, (slip st in next ch-1 sp, ch 2) across to next corner; repeat from ★ around; join with slip st to first slip st, finish off.

Holding 7 strands of yarn together, add fringe evenly across short edges of Afghan *(Figs. 27a & b, page 126)*.

HOUSEWARMING

*Love makes a house
a home — and lacy hearts
make this afghan a warming gift.
It's just the thing for friends
who've recently moved
into a new home.*

HEART SILHOUETTES

Finished Size: 53" x 65"

MATERIALS
Worsted Weight Yarn:
38½ ounces, (1,090 grams, 2,640 yards)
Crochet hook, size I (5.50 mm) **or** size needed
for gauge
Yarn needle

GAUGE: Each Square = 12½"

Gauge Swatch: 4"
Work same as Square Rnds 1-3.

SQUARE (Make 20)
Rnd 1 (Right side): Ch 4, 2 dc in fourth ch from hook
(3 skipped chs count as first dc), ch 3, (3 dc in same ch,
ch 3) 3 times; join with slip st to first dc: 12 dc and
4 ch-3 sps.
Note: Loop a short piece of yarn around any stitch to
mark Rnd 1 as **right** side.
Rnd 2: Ch 3 **(counts as first dc, now and throughout)**,
dc in next 2 dc, (2 dc, ch 3, 2 dc) in next ch-3 sp,
★ dc in next 3 dc, (2 dc, ch 3, 2 dc) in next ch-3 sp;
repeat from ★ 2 times **more**; join with slip st to first dc:
28 dc and 4 ch-3 sps.

Rnd 3: Ch 4 **(counts as first dc plus ch 1, now and
throughout)**, skip next dc, dc in next 3 dc, (2 dc, ch 3,
2 dc) in next corner ch-3 sp, ★ dc in next 3 dc, ch 1, skip
next dc, dc in next 3 dc, (2 dc, ch 3, 2 dc) in next corner
ch-3 sp; repeat from ★ 2 times **more**, dc in last 2 dc; join
with slip st to first dc: 40 dc and 8 sps.
Rnd 4: Ch 4, dc in next dc, ch 1, skip next dc, dc in next
3 dc, (2 dc, ch 3, 2 dc) in next corner ch-3 sp, dc in next
3 dc, ch 1, skip next dc, ★ (dc in next dc, ch 1) twice, skip
next dc, dc in next 3 dc, (2 dc, ch 3, 2 dc) in next corner
ch-3 sp, dc in next 3 dc, ch 1, skip next dc; repeat from ★
2 times **more**; join with slip st to first dc: 48 dc and 16 sps.
Rnd 5: Ch 4, (dc in next dc, ch 1) twice, skip next dc, dc
in next 3 dc, (2 dc, ch 3, 2 dc) in next corner ch-3 sp, dc
in next 3 dc, ch 1, skip next dc, ★ (dc in next dc, ch 1) 4
times, skip next dc, dc in next 3 dc, (2 dc, ch 3, 2 dc) in
next corner ch-3 sp, dc in next 3 dc, ch 1, skip next dc;
repeat from ★ 2 times **more**, dc in last dc, ch 1; join with
slip st to first dc: 56 dc and 24 sps.
Rnd 6: Ch 4, (dc in next dc, ch 1) 3 times, skip next dc,
dc in next 3 dc, (2 dc, ch 3, 2 dc) in next corner ch-3 sp,
dc in next 3 dc, ch 1, skip next dc, ★ (dc in next dc, ch 1)
6 times, skip next dc, dc in next 3 dc, (2 dc, ch 3, 2 dc) in
next corner ch-3 sp, dc in next 3 dc, ch 1, skip next dc;
repeat from ★ 2 times **more**, (dc in next dc, ch 1) twice;
join with slip st to first dc: 64 dc and 32 sps.
Rnd 7: Ch 4, (dc in next dc, ch 1) 4 times, skip next dc,
dc in next 3 dc, (2 dc, ch 3, 2 dc) in next corner ch-3 sp,
dc in next 3 dc, ch 1, skip next dc, ★ (dc in next dc, ch 1)
8 times, skip next dc, dc in next 3 dc, (2 dc, ch 3, 2 dc) in
next corner ch-3 sp, dc in next 3 dc, ch 1, skip next dc;
repeat from ★ 2 times **more**, (dc in next dc, ch 1) 3 times;
join with slip st to first dc: 72 dc and 40 sps.
Rnd 8: Ch 4, (dc in next dc, ch 1) 4 times, dc in next
5 dc, ch 1, (dc, ch 3, dc) in next corner ch-3 sp, ch 1, dc
in next 5 dc, ch 1, ★ (dc in next dc, ch 1) 8 times, dc in
next 5 dc, ch 1, (dc, ch 3, dc) in next corner ch-3 sp, ch 1,
dc in next 5 dc, ch 1; repeat from ★ 2 times **more**, (dc in
next dc, ch 1) 3 times; join with slip st to first dc: 80 dc
and 48 sps.
Rnd 9: Ch 3, dc in next ch-1 sp, (dc in next dc, ch 1) 4
times, dc in next 5 dc, ch 1, dc in next dc, ch 1, (dc, ch 3,
dc) in next corner ch-3 sp, ★ † ch 1, dc in next dc, ch 1,
dc in next 5 dc, ch 1, (dc in next dc, ch 1) 3 times †, dc in
next dc and in next ch-1 sp, (dc in next dc, ch 1) 4 times,
dc in next 5 dc, ch 1, dc in next dc, ch 1, (dc, ch 3, dc) in
next corner ch-3 sp; repeat from ★ 2 times **more**, then
repeat from † to † once; join with slip st to first dc, do **not**
finish off: 92 dc and 52 sps.

Instructions continued on page 113.

GET WELL SOON

Brighten the day for a friend who's feeling under the weather with this beautiful afghan and matching pillow. The design was inspired by intricate Moroccan mosaics.

MOROCCAN TILE

Finished Size: 50" x 69"

MATERIALS

Worsted Weight Yarn:
 Ecru - 13 ounces, (370 grams, 890 yards)
 Tan - 12 ounces, (340 grams, 825 yards)
 Maroon - 6 ounces, (170 grams, 410 yards)
 Lt Blue - 3 ounces, (90 grams, 205 yards)
 Blue - 7 ounces, (200 grams, 480 yards)
 Dk Blue - 6 ounces, (170 grams, 410 yards)
Crochet hook, size J (6.00 mm) **or** size needed for gauge
Yarn needle

GAUGE: Each Square = 9¼"

Gauge Swatch: 5" square
Work same as Square through Rnd 5.

STITCH GUIDE

> **CLUSTER**
> ★ YO, insert hook in st indicated, YO and pull up a loop, YO and draw through 2 loops on hook; repeat from ★ once **more**, YO and draw through all 3 loops on hook *(Figs. 16a & b, page 124)*.
>
> **DECREASE**
> Pull up a loop in next 2 sc, YO and draw through all 3 loops on hook **(counts as one sc)**.

SQUARE A (Make 18)

With Maroon, ch 4; join with slip st to form a ring.

Rnd 1 (Right side): Ch 4, dc in ring, ch 2, (dc in ring, ch 1, dc in ring, ch 2) 3 times; join with slip st to third ch of beginning ch-4: 8 sps.

Note: Loop a short piece of yarn around any stitch to mark Rnd 1 as **right** side.

Rnd 2: Slip st in first ch-1 sp, ch 1, 3 sc in same sp, 5 sc in next ch-2 sp, (3 sc in next ch-1 sp, 5 sc in next ch-2 sp) around; join with slip st to first sc, finish off: 32 sc.

Rnd 3: With **right** side facing, join Lt Blue with slip st in center sc of any 3-sc group; ch 2, dc in same st, skip next 3 sc, work (Cluster, ch 4, Cluster) in next sc, ★ skip next 3 sc, work (Cluster, ch 3, Cluster) in next sc, skip next 3 sc, work (Cluster, ch 4, Cluster) in next sc; repeat from ★ 2 times **more**, skip last 3 sc, work Cluster in same st as beginning ch-2, ch 3, skip beginning ch-2 and join with slip st to first dc, finish off: 16 Clusters.

Rnd 4: With **right** side facing, join Blue with slip st in first st; ch 1, sc in same st and in next Cluster, 5 sc in next ch-4 sp, sc in next 2 Clusters, 3 sc in next ch-3 sp, ★ sc in next 2 Clusters, 5 sc in next ch-4 sp, sc in next 2 Clusters, 3 sc in next ch-3 sp; repeat from ★ around; join with slip st to first sc, finish off: 48 sc.

Rnd 5: With **right** side facing and working in Back Loops Only *(Fig. 20, page 125)*, join Dk Blue with slip st in center sc of any 5-sc group; ch 4 **(counts as first tr)**, (tr, ch 2, 2 tr) in same st, tr in next 11 sc, ★ (2 tr, ch 2, 2 tr) in next sc, tr in next 11 sc; repeat from ★ around; join with slip st to first tr, finish off: 60 tr.

Rnd 6: With **right** side facing and working in both loops, join Tan with slip st in fourth tr to **right** of any corner ch-2 sp; ★ skip next 3 tr, tr in corner ch-2 sp, (ch 1, tr) 7 times in same sp, skip next 3 tr, slip st in next tr, skip next 3 tr, tr in next tr, (ch 1, tr) 5 times in same st, skip next 3 tr, slip st in next tr; repeat from ★ around working last slip st in first slip st, finish off: 56 tr.

Note: Work next 3 rounds in Back Loops Only.

Rnd 7: With **right** side facing, join Blue with slip st in center ch of any corner; ch 1, 2 sc in same st, sc in next tr, (2 sc in next ch, sc in next tr) twice, ★ † sc in next ch, skip next 2 tr, sc in next ch and in next tr, (2 sc in next ch, sc in next tr) 3 times, sc in next ch, skip next 2 tr, sc in next ch and in next tr †, (2 sc in next ch, sc in next tr) 5 times; repeat from ★ 2 times **more**, then repeat from † to † once, (2 sc in next ch, sc in next tr) twice; join with slip st to first sc, finish off: 120 sc.

Rnd 8: With **right** side facing, join Maroon with slip st in first sc; ch 1, sc in same st and in next 8 sc, ★ † skip next 2 sc, sc in next 10 sc, skip next 2 sc †, sc in next 16 sc; repeat from ★ 2 times **more**, then repeat from † to † once, sc in last 7 sc; join with slip st to first sc, finish off: 104 sc.

Instructions continued on page 114.

IN THE PINK

*Keep in touch with an
old friend by sending
this lovely afghan.
Wrapped in its rosy
rows, your friend will
always be "in the pink!"*

ROSE GLOW

Finished Size: 45" x 62"

MATERIALS
Worsted Weight Yarn:
  Dk Pink - 13½ ounces, (380 grams, 880 yards)
  Pink - 13 ounces, (370 grams, 850 yards)
  Lt Pink - 13 ounces, (370 grams, 850 yards)
  Crochet hook, size J (6.00 mm) **or** size needed
    for gauge

GAUGE: In pattern, (7 dc, sc) 3 times = 5";
        8 rows = 4"

Gauge Swatch: 5¼"w x 4"h
With Dk Pink, ch 20 **loosely**.
Work same as Afghan for 8 rows.
Finish off.

AFGHAN
With Dk Pink, ch 164 **loosely**.
Row 1: Sc in second ch from hook and in each ch across:
163 sc.
Row 2 (Right side): Ch 1, turn; sc in first sc, ★ skip next
2 sc, 7 dc in next sc, skip next 2 sc, sc in next sc; repeat
from ★ across changing to Pink in last sc (*Fig. 22a,
page 125*): 189 dc and 28 sc.

Row 3: Ch 4 (**counts as first tr, now and throughout**),
turn; skip next dc, dc in next 5 dc, ★ ch 1, skip next 3 sts,
dc in next 5 dc; repeat from ★ across to last 2 sts, skip next
dc, tr in last sc changing to Lt Pink: 137 sts and 26 ch-1 sps.
Row 4: Ch 3 (**counts as first dc, now and throughout**),
turn; 3 dc in same st, skip next 2 dc, sc in next dc, ★ skip
next 2 dc, 7 dc in next ch-1 sp, skip next 2 dc, sc in next
dc; repeat from ★ across to last 3 sts, skip next 2 dc, 4 dc in
last tr changing to Dk Pink in last dc: 190 dc and 27 sc.
Row 5: Ch 3, turn; dc in next 2 dc, ch 1, ★ skip next 3 sts,
dc in next 5 dc, ch 1; repeat from ★ across to last 6 sts,
skip next 3 sts, dc in last 3 dc changing to Pink in last dc:
136 dc and 27 ch-1 sps.
Row 6: Ch 1, turn; sc in first dc, ★ skip next 2 dc, 7 dc in
next ch-1 sp, skip next 2 dc, sc in next dc; repeat from ★
across changing to Lt Pink in last sc: 189 dc and 28 sc.
Row 7: Ch 4, turn; skip next dc, dc in next 5 dc, ★ ch 1,
skip next 3 sts, dc in next 5 dc; repeat from ★ across to
last 2 sts, skip next dc, tr in last sc changing to Dk Pink:
137 sts and 26 ch-1 sps.
Row 8: Ch 3, turn; 3 dc in same st, skip next 2 dc, sc in
next dc, ★ skip next 2 dc, 7 dc in next ch-1 sp, skip next
2 dc, sc in next dc; repeat from ★ across to last 3 sts,
skip next 2 dc, 4 dc in last tr changing to Pink in last dc:
190 dc and 27 sc.
Row 9: Ch 3, turn; dc in next 2 dc, ch 1, ★ skip next 3 sts,
dc in next 5 dc, ch 1; repeat from ★ across to last 6 sts, skip
next 3 sts, dc in last 3 dc changing to Lt Pink in last dc:
136 dc and 27 ch-1 sps.
Row 10: Ch 1, turn; sc in first dc, ★ skip next 2 dc, 7 dc in
next ch-1 sp, skip next 2 dc, sc in next dc; repeat from ★
across changing to Dk Pink in last sc: 189 dc and 28 sc.
Row 11: Ch 4, turn; skip next dc, dc in next 5 dc, ★ ch 1,
skip next 3 sts, dc in next 5 dc; repeat from ★ across to
last 2 sts, skip next dc, tr in last sc changing to Pink:
137 sts and 26 ch-1 sps.
Row 12: Ch 3, turn; 3 dc in same st, skip next 2 dc, sc in
next dc, ★ skip next 2 dc, 7 dc in next ch-1 sp, skip next
2 dc, sc in next dc; repeat from ★ across to last 3 sts, skip
next 2 dc, 4 dc in last tr changing to Lt Pink in last dc:
190 dc and 27 sc.
Row 13: Ch 3, turn; dc in next 2 dc, ch 1, ★ skip next
3 sts, dc in next 5 dc, ch 1; repeat from ★ across to last
6 sts, skip next 3 sts, dc in last 3 dc changing to Dk Pink in
last dc: 136 dc and 27 ch-1 sps.
Row 14: Ch 1, turn; sc in first dc, ★ skip next 2 dc, 7 dc in
next ch-1 sp, skip next 2 dc, sc in next dc; repeat from ★
across changing to Pink in last sc: 189 dc and 28 sc.
Rows 15-122: Repeat Rows 3-14, 9 times; at end of
Row 122, do **not** change colors.
Row 123: With Dk Pink, ch 1, turn; sc in first dc
and in each st across; finish off.

FOR A BABY BOY

A thoughtful shower gift, this precious afghan will wrap a newborn son in the warmth of handmade love. I love this pattern because the soft strips work up so quickly.

LITTLE BOY BLUE

Finished Size: 36" x 47"

MATERIALS
Sport Weight Yarn:
    White - 16 ounces, (450 grams, 1,280 yards)
    Blue - 15 ounces, (430 grams, 1,200 yards)
    Crochet hook, size F (3.75 mm) **or** size needed
      for gauge

GAUGE SWATCH: 1"w x 4"h
Work same as Center through Row 11.
Finish off.

STITCH GUIDE
CLUSTER (uses one st)
★ YO, insert hook in st indicated, YO and pull up a loop, YO and draw through 2 loops on hook; repeat from ★ 2 times **more**, YO and draw through all 4 loops on hook *(Figs. 16a & b, page 124)*.
DC DECREASE (uses next 2 sc)
★ YO, insert hook in **next** sc, YO and pull up a loop, YO and draw through 2 loops on hook; repeat from ★ once **more**, YO and draw through all 3 loops on hook **(counts as one dc)**.
SC DECREASE (uses next 3 sc)
Pull up a loop in next 3 sc, YO and draw through all 4 loops on hook **(counts as one sc)**.

FIRST STRIP
CENTER
With Blue, ch 8 **loosely**.
Row 1 (Right side): Work Cluster in seventh ch from hook, ch 1, tr in last ch: one Cluster.
Note: Loop a short piece of yarn around any stitch to mark Row 1 as **right** side and bottom edge.
Row 2: Ch 1, turn; skip first tr, sc in next ch-1 sp, skip next Cluster, 2 sc in next sp: 3 sc.
Row 3: Ch 5 **(counts as first tr plus ch 1)**, turn; work Cluster in next sc, ch 1, tr in last sc: 3 sts and 2 ch-1 sps.
Rows 4-120: Repeat Rows 2 and 3, 58 times; then repeat Row 2 once **more**.
Finish off.

BORDER
Rnd 1: With **right** side facing, join White with slip st in first sc on Row 120; ch 1, 3 sc in same st, ch 5, slip st in top of last sc made *(Fig. 25, page 126)*, sc in next sc, ch 5, slip st in top of sc just made, 3 sc in last sc; working in end of rows, skip first row, 5 sc in next row, (skip next row, 5 sc in next row) across; working in free loops of beginning ch *(Fig. 21b, page 125)*, 3 sc in first ch, ch 5, slip st in top of last sc made, sc in next ch, ch 5, slip st in top of sc just made, 3 sc in next ch; working in end of rows, 5 sc in first row, skip next row, (5 sc in next row, skip next row) across; join with slip st to first sc: 614 sc and 4 ch-5 sps.
Rnd 2: Ch 2, dc in next sc, † ch 3, 5 sc in next ch-5 sp, dc in next sc, 5 sc in next ch-5 sp, ch 3, skip next sc, dc decrease, ch 3, skip next sc, sc decrease, ch 3, (skip next 2 sc, sc decrease, ch 3) 59 times, skip next sc †, dc decrease, repeat from † to † once; join with slip st to first dc, finish off: 146 sts and 126 ch-3 sps.
Rnd 3: With **right** side facing, join Blue with slip st in first ch-3 sp; ch 1, (2 sc, hdc, dc) in same sp, place marker in last dc made for st placement, dc in same sp, † skip next sc, sc in next 3 sc, skip next sc, 3 dc in next dc, skip next sc, sc in next 3 sc, (2 dc, hdc, 2 sc) in next ch-3 sp, 3 dc in each of next 61 ch-3 sps †, (2 sc, hdc, 2 dc) in next ch-3 sp, repeat from † to † once; join with slip st to first sc, finish off: 404 sts.
Rnd 4: With **right** side facing, join White with slip st in marked dc, remove marker; ch 1, (sc, ch 3, sc) in same st, † ★ skip next 2 sts, dc in next sc, (ch 1, dc in same st) 3 times, skip next 2 sts, (sc, ch 3, sc) in next dc; repeat from ★ once **more**, slip st in next hdc, [skip next st, (sc, ch 3, sc) in next st, skip next st, slip st in next st] 47 times †, (sc, ch 3, sc) in next dc, repeat from † to † once; join with slip st to first sc, finish off.

Instructions continued on page 115.

GRANDPARENTS DAY

Grandmother and Grandfather will adore this old-fashioned wrap! It's assembled from simple-to-make granny squares worked in homey colors.

VICTORIAN GRANNY

Finished Size: 48" x 62"

MATERIALS
Worsted Weight Yarn:
    Black - 19 ounces, (540 grams, 1,305 yards)
    Lt Green - 7½ ounces, (210 grams, 515 yards)
    Lt Rose - 7½ ounces, (210 grams, 515 yards)
    Green - 6 ounces, (170 grams, 410 yards)
    Rose - 6 ounces, (170 grams, 410 yards)
Crochet hook, size I (5.50 mm) **or** size needed
    for gauge
Yarn needle

GAUGE: Each Square = 6¾"

Gauge Swatch: 3¾"
Work same as Square A or B Rnds 1-3.

SQUARES A AND B
Referring to table below, make the number of Squares specified in the colors indicated.

	Square A Make 24	Square B Make 24
Rnd 1	Green	Rose
Rnd 2	Lt Green	Lt Rose
Rnd 3	Black	Black
Rnd 4	Rose	Green
Rnd 5	Lt Rose	Lt Green
Rnd 6	Black	Black

Rnd 1 (Right side): With color indicated, ch 4, 2 dc in fourth ch from hook, ch 3, (3 dc in same ch, ch 3) 3 times; join with slip st to top of beginning ch-4, finish off: 4 ch-3 sps.
Note: Loop a short piece of yarn around any stitch to mark Rnd 1 as **right** side.
Rnd 2: With **right** side facing, join next color with slip st in any ch-3 sp; ch 3 **(counts as first dc, now and throughout)**, (2 dc, ch 3, 3 dc) in same sp, ch 1, ★ (3 dc, ch 3, 3 dc) in next ch-3 sp, ch 1; repeat from ★ 2 times **more**; join with slip st to first dc, finish off: 24 dc and 8 sps.
Rnd 3: With **right** side facing, join Black with slip st in any corner ch-3 sp; ch 3, (2 dc, ch 3, 3 dc) in same sp, ch 1, 3 dc in next ch-1 sp, ch 1, ★ (3 dc, ch 3, 3 dc) in next corner ch-3 sp, ch 1, 3 dc in next ch-1 sp, ch 1; repeat from ★ 2 times **more**; join with slip st to first dc, finish off: 36 dc and 12 sps.
Rnds 4-6: With **right** side facing, join next color with slip st in any corner ch-3 sp; ch 3, (2 dc, ch 3, 3 dc) in same sp, ch 1, (3 dc in next ch-1 sp, ch 1) across to next corner ch-3 sp, ★ (3 dc, ch 3, 3 dc) in next corner ch-3 sp, ch 1, (3 dc in next ch-1 sp, ch 1) across to next corner ch-3 sp; repeat from ★ 2 times **more**; join with slip st to first dc, finish off: 72 dc and 24 sps.

ASSEMBLY
With Black, using Placement Diagram, page 115, as a guide, and working through both loops, whipstitch Squares together *(Fig. 26b, page 126)*, forming 6 vertical strips of 8 Squares each, beginning in center ch of first corner ch-3 and ending in center ch of next corner ch-3; whipstitch strips together in same manner.

Instructions continued on page 115.

WHILE YOU RECOVER

As your neighbor recovers from a hospital stay, offer a little comfort with a plush wrap. The thick throw works up quickly, so it will be ready to lift spirits in no time!

PLUSH COMFORT

Finished Size: 47" x 67"

MATERIALS
    Worsted Weight Yarn:
        35½ ounces, (1,010 grams, 2,740 yards)
    Crochet hook, size Q (15.00 mm)
    Yarn needle

Note: Afghan is worked holding two strands of yarn together throughout.

GAUGE: Each Center = 12" wide;
            Rows 1-8 = 8"

Gauge Swatch: 5"w x 8"h
Ch 9 **loosely.**
Row 1: Sc in second ch from hook and in each ch across: 8 sc.
Row 2: Ch 3, turn; dc in next sc and in each sc across.
Row 3: Ch 1, turn; sc in each st across.
Rows 4-8: Repeat Rows 2 and 3 twice, then repeat Row 2 once **more.**
Finish off.

STITCH GUIDE

POPCORN
Work 4 dc in sc indicated, drop loop from hook, insert hook in first dc of 4-dc group, hook dropped loop and draw through *(Fig. 18, page 124).*
V-STITCH *(abbreviated V-St)*
(Dc, ch 1, dc) in st or sp indicated.

PANEL (Make 3)
CENTER
Ch 20 **loosely.**
Row 1: Sc in second ch from hook and in each ch across: 19 sc.
Row 2 (Right side): Ch 3 **(counts as first dc, now and throughout)**, turn; dc in next sc and in each sc across.
Note: Loop a short piece of yarn around any stitch to mark Row 2 as **right** side and bottom edge.
Row 3: Ch 1, turn; sc in each dc across.
Row 4: Ch 3, turn; dc in next 7 sc, ch 1, skip next sc, work Popcorn in next sc, ch 1, skip next sc, dc in last 8 sc: 16 dc and one Popcorn.
Row 5: Ch 1, turn; sc in each st and in each ch-1 sp across: 19 sc.
Row 6: Ch 3, turn; dc in next 5 sc, ch 1, skip next sc, work Popcorn in next sc, ch 1, skip next sc, dc in next sc, ch 1, skip next sc, work Popcorn in next sc, ch 1, skip next sc, dc in last 6 sc: 13 dc and 2 Popcorns.
Row 7: Ch 1, turn; sc in each st and in each ch-1 sp across: 19 sc.
Row 8: Ch 3, turn; dc in next 3 sc, ch 1, skip next sc, work Popcorn in next sc, ch 1, skip next sc, ★ dc in next sc, ch 1, skip next sc, work Popcorn in next sc, ch 1, skip next sc; repeat from ★ once **more**, dc in last 4 sc: 10 dc and 3 Popcorns.
Rows 9-11: Repeat Rows 5-7.
Rows 12 and 13: Repeat Rows 4 and 5.
Row 14: Ch 3, turn; dc in next sc and in each sc across.
Row 15: Ch 1, turn; sc in each dc across.
Rows 16-63: Repeat Rows 4-15, 4 times.
Do **not** finish off.

BORDER
Ch 4 **(counts as first dc plus ch 1, now and throughout)**, turn; work V-St in same st, (skip next 2 sc, work V-St in next sc) across to last 3 sc, skip next 2 sc, (work V-St, ch 1, dc) in last sc; † working in end of rows, skip first row, (work V-St in next row, skip next row) across †; working in free loops of beginning ch *(Fig. 21b, page 125)*, (work V-St, ch 1, dc) in ch at base of first sc, (skip next 2 chs, work V-St in next ch) across to last 3 chs, skip next 2 chs, (work V-St, ch 1, dc) in last ch, repeat from † to † once; join with slip st to first dc, finish off.

Instructions continued on page 116.

SCHOOL DAYS

This "a-peel-ing"
duo will win
high marks
with a favorite
teacher who loves
country touches!

COUNTRY CHECKS

Finished Size: 47" x 61"

MATERIALS
Worsted Weight Yarn:
    Ecru - 21 ounces, (600 grams, 1,440 yards)
    Red - 21 ounces, (600 grams, 1,440 yards)
    Crochet hook, size I (5.50 mm) **or** size needed for gauge

GAUGE: 14 dc and 8 rows = 4"

Gauge Swatch: 4¹/₄"w x 4"h
With Ecru, ch 17 **loosely**.
Work same as Afghan Body for 8 rows.
Finish off.

Note: Each row is worked across length of Afghan.

AFGHAN BODY
With Ecru, ch 209 **loosely**, place marker in third ch from hook for st placement.
Note: Carry unused yarn **loosely** across **wrong** side of work, do **not** cut yarn unless otherwise specified. When working **next** row, work **over** carried strand.
Row 1 (Right side): Dc in fourth ch from hook **(3 skipped chs count as first dc)**, dc in next ch changing to Red **(Fig. 22a, page 125)**, dc in next 3 chs changing to Ecru in last dc, ★ dc in next 3 chs changing to Red in last dc, dc in next 3 chs changing to Ecru in last dc; repeat from ★ across to last 3 chs, dc in last 3 chs: 207 dc.

Note #1: Loop a short piece of yarn around any stitch to mark Row 1 as **right** side.
Note #2: Continue changing colors in same manner throughout.
Row 2: Ch 3 **(counts as first dc, now and throughout)**, turn; dc in next 2 dc, (with Red dc in next 3 dc, with Ecru dc in next 3 dc) across changing to Red in last dc.
Row 3: Ch 3, turn; dc in next 2 dc, (with Ecru dc in next 3 dc, with Red dc in next 3 dc) across.
Row 4: Ch 3, turn; dc in next 2 dc, (with Ecru dc in next 3 dc, with Red dc in next 3 dc) across changing to Ecru in last dc.
Row 5: Ch 3, turn; dc in next 2 dc, (with Red dc in next 3 dc, with Ecru dc in next 3 dc) across.
Row 6: Ch 3, turn; dc in next 2 dc, (with Red dc in next 3 dc, with Ecru dc in next 3 dc) across changing to Red in last dc.
Rows 7-90: Repeat Rows 3-6, 21 times; at end of Row 90, do **not** change colors; cut Red.

EDGING
Rnd 1: Ch 1, turn; sc in each dc across to last dc, 3 sc in last dc; 2 sc in end of each row across; working in free loops of beginning ch **(Fig. 21b, page 125)**, 3 sc in first ch, 2 sc in next ch, sc in each ch across to marked ch, 3 sc in marked ch; 2 sc in end of each row across and in same st as first sc; join with slip st to first sc: 783 sc.
Rnd 2: Ch 1, sc in same st, ch 4, skip next 2 sc, ★ sc in next sc, ch 4, skip next 2 sc; repeat from ★ around; join with slip st to first sc, finish off.
Rnd 3: With **right** side facing, join Red with slip st in any ch-4 sp; ch 4, ★ drop loop from hook, insert hook from front to back in next ch-4 sp, hook dropped loop and draw through ch-4 sp, ch 4; repeat from ★ around; join with slip st to first slip st, finish off.

APPLE PILLOW

Finished Size: 14¹/₂"w x 15¹/₂"h

MATERIALS
Worsted Weight Yarn:
    Red - 9 ounces, (260 grams, 615 yards)
    Green - 20 yards
    Brown - 14 yards
    Crochet hook, size N (9.00 mm) **or** size needed for gauge
    Yarn needle
    Polyester fiberfill

Instructions continued on page 116.

WARM WISHES

When it's time to chase away the winter chills, give this warming duo! I couldn't resist trying out the cozy booties that go with this stylish striped wrap.

STYLISH STRIPES

Finished Size: 50½" x 71"

MATERIALS
Worsted Weight Yarn:
  Ecru - 21 ounces, (600 grams, 1,380 yards)
  Lt Blue - 19 ounces, (540 grams, 1,250 yards)
  Blue - 6½ ounces, (180 grams, 420 yards)
Crochet hook, size I (5.50 mm) **or** size needed for gauge

GAUGE: In pattern, (2 sc, ch 2) 4 times and 15 rows = 4"

Gauge Swatch: 4½" w x 4"h
Ch 19 **loosely.**
Work same as Afghan Body for 15 rows.
Finish off.

COLOR SEQUENCE
One row **each** of Ecru, Lt Blue, Ecru, Blue, Ecru, Lt Blue, 2 rows Ecru, ★ 1 row **each** of Lt Blue, Blue, Lt Blue, 2 rows Ecru, 1 row Lt Blue, 2 rows Ecru, 1 row **each** of Lt Blue, Blue, 3 rows Lt Blue, 1 row **each** of Blue, Lt Blue, 2 rows Ecru, 1 row Lt Blue, 2 rows Ecru, 1 row **each** of Lt Blue, Blue, Lt Blue, 2 rows Ecru, 1 row **each** of Lt Blue, Ecru, Blue, Ecru, Lt Blue, 2 rows Ecru; repeat from ★ 7 times **more.**

AFGHAN BODY
With Ecru, ch 203 **loosely.**
Row 1 (Right side): Sc in second ch from hook and in next ch, (ch 2, skip next 2 chs, sc in next 2 chs) across changing to Lt Blue in last sc *(Fig. 22a, page 125)*: 102 sc.
Note: Loop a short piece of yarn around any stitch to mark Row 1 as **right** side.
Rows 2-264: Ch 1, turn; sc in first 2 sc, (ch 2, sc in next 2 sc) across.
Do **not** finish off.

EDGING
TOP
Turn; slip st in first 2 sc, (ch 3, slip st in next 2 sc) across; finish off.

BOTTOM
With **right** side facing and working in free loops of beginning ch *(Fig. 21b, page 125)*, join Ecru with slip st in first ch; slip st in next ch, (ch 3, skip next 2 chs, slip st in next 2 chs) 50 times; finish off.

WOMEN'S BOOTIES

Size:	Small	Medium	Large
Fits Shoe Sizes:	5/6	7/8	9/10

Size Note: Instructions are written for size Small with sizes Medium and Large in braces { }. Instructions will be easier to read if you circle all the numbers pertaining to your size. If only one number is given, it applies to all sizes.

MATERIALS
Worsted Weight Yarn: 3¼{3½ -3¾} ounces, [95{100-105} grams, 185{210-225} yards]
Crochet hook, size G (4.00 mm) {H (5.00 mm) - I (5.50 mm)} **or** size needed for gauge
Yarn needle

GAUGE: 8{7-6} sc and 9{8-7} rows = 2"

Gauge Swatch: 2" square
Ch 9{8-7} **loosely.**
Row 1: Sc in second ch from hook and in each ch across: 8{7-6} sc.
Rows 2 thru 9{8-7}: Ch 1, turn; sc in each sc across.
Finish off.

Instructions continued on page 117.

84

ROSES ARE RED

Your valentine will fall in love with this romantic cover-up, which embodies a fond childhood verse. This token of affection is graced with dimensional roses and violets.

ROMANTIC COVER-UP

Finished Size: 48" x 66"

MATERIALS
Worsted Weight Yarn:
    Ecru - 41 ounces, (1,160 grams, 2,810 yards)
    Red - 6 ounces, (170 grams, 375 yards)
    Green - 5 ounces, (140 grams, 345 yards)
    Purple - 5 ounces, (140 grams, 345 yards)
Crochet hooks, sizes G (4.00 mm) **and** I (5.50 mm) **or** sizes needed for gauge
Yarn needle

GAUGE: With large size hook, in pattern,
        7 Cross Sts = 5" and 10 rows = 3½"

Gauge Swatch: 5½"w x 3½"h
With Ecru and large size hook, ch 24 **loosely**.
Work same as Afghan Body for 10 rows.
Finish off.

STITCH GUIDE

CROSS STITCH *(abbreviated Cross St)*
Skip next 2 sc, dc in next sc, ch 1, working **around** dc just made, dc in first skipped sc *(Fig. 1)*.

Fig. 1

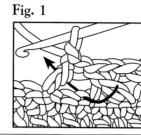

AFGHAN BODY
With Ecru and large size hook, ch 102 **loosely**.
Row 1 (Right side)**:** Sc in second ch from hook and in each ch across: 101 sc.
Note: Loop a short piece of yarn around any stitch to mark Row 1 as **right** side and bottom edge.
Row 2: Ch 3 **(counts as first dc, now and throughout)**, turn; work Cross St across to last sc, dc in last sc: 33 Cross Sts.
Row 3: Ch 1, turn; sc in each dc and in each ch-1 sp across
Repeat Rows 2 and 3 for pattern until Afghan measures approximately 42", ending by working Row 3, do **not** finish off.

EDGING
Rnd 1: Ch 1, 2 sc in same st, work 143 sc evenly spaced across end of rows; working in free loops of beginning ch *(Fig. 21b, page 125)*, 3 sc in first ch, work 81 sc evenly spaced across to last ch, 3 sc in last ch; work 143 sc evenly spaced across end of rows; 3 sc in first st, work 81 sc evenly spaced across last row, sc in same st as first sc; join with slip st to first sc: 460 sc.
Rnd 2: Ch 1, 3 sc in same st, sc in each sc around working 3 sc in each corner sc; join with slip st to first sc, finish off: 468 sc.
Rnd 3: With **right** side facing, join Green with slip st in any corner sc; ch 3, dc in same st, dc in next sc and in each sc across to next corner sc, ★ (2 dc, ch 1, 2 dc) in corner sc, dc in next sc and in each sc across to next corner sc; repeat from ★ around, 2 dc in same st as first dc, ch 1; join with slip st to first dc, finish off: 480 dc.
Rnd 4: With **right** side facing, join Ecru with slip st in any corner ch-1 sp; ch 4 **(counts as first dc plus ch 1, now and throughout)**, 2 dc in same sp, dc in each dc across to next corner ch-1 sp, ★ (2 dc, ch 1, 2 dc) in corner ch-1 sp, dc in each dc across to next corner ch-1 sp; repeat from ★ around, dc in same sp as first dc; join with slip st to first dc: 496 dc.
Rnds 5 and 6: Slip st in first ch-1 sp, ch 4, 2 dc in same sp, dc in each dc across to next corner ch-1 sp, ★ (2 dc, ch 1, 2 dc) in corner ch-1 sp, dc in each dc across to next corner ch-1 sp; repeat from ★ around, dc in same sp as first dc; join with slip st to first dc; do **not** finish off: 528 dc.

Instructions continued on page 118.

ST. PATRICK'S DAY

On St. Patrick's Day, there's no better way to celebrate a friend's Irish heritage than with this lush emerald afghan. The clover-strewn wrap offers many blessings!

EMERALD ISLE

Finished Size: 52" x 69½"

MATERIALS
Worsted Weight Yarn:
  Lt Green - 19 ounces, (540 grams, 1,275 yards)
  Green - 23 ounces, (650 grams, 1,545 yards)
  Dk Green - 14 ounces, (400 grams, 940 yards)
Crochet hook, size H (5.00 mm) **or** size needed
  for gauge
Yarn needle

GAUGE SWATCH: 5¾"
Work same as Square.

SQUARE (Make 108)
With Lt Green, ch 6; join with slip st to form a ring.
Rnd 1 (Right side): Ch 3 **(counts as first dc, now and throughout)**, 3 dc in ring, ch 2, (4 dc in ring, ch 2) 3 times; join with slip st to first dc, finish off: 16 dc.
Note: Loop a short piece of yarn around any stitch to mark Rnd 1 as **right** side.
Rnd 2: With **right** side facing, join Green with slip st in any ch-2 sp; ch 3, (2 dc, ch 1, 3 dc) in same sp, (skip next dc, dc in sp **before** next dc) 3 times *(Fig. 23, page 125)*, ★ (3 dc, ch 1, 3 dc) in next corner ch-2 sp, (skip next dc, dc in sp **before** next dc) 3 times; repeat from ★ around; join with slip st to first dc, finish off: 36 dc.
Rnd 3: With **right** side facing, join Dk Green with slip st in any corner ch-1 sp; ch 4 **(counts as first tr)**, (4 tr, ch 2, 5 tr) in same sp, skip next 2 dc, sc in next 5 dc, skip next 2 dc, ★ (5 tr, ch 2, 5 tr) in next corner ch-1 sp, skip next 2 dc, sc in next 5 dc, skip next 2 dc; repeat from ★ around; join with slip st to first tr, finish off: 15 sts **each** side.
Rnd 4: With **right** side facing, join Lt Green with slip st in any corner ch-2 sp; ch 2, (2 hdc, ch 1, 3 hdc) in same sp, ★ † hdc in next 2 tr, dc in next 3 tr, tr in next 2 sc, skip next sc, tr in next 2 sc, dc in next 3 tr, hdc in next 2 tr †, (3 hdc, ch 1, 3 hdc) in next corner ch-2 sp; repeat from ★ 2 times **more**, then repeat from † to † once; join with slip st to top of beginning ch-2, finish off: 20 sts **each** side.
Rnd 5: With **right** side facing, join Green with slip st in any corner ch-1 sp; ch 3, (dc, ch 1, 2 dc) in same sp, ch 1, (skip next st, dc in next st, ch 1) across to next corner ch-1 sp, ★ (2 dc, ch 1, 2 dc) in corner ch-1 sp, ch 1, (skip next st, dc in next st, ch 1) across to next corner ch-1 sp; repeat from ★ around; join with slip st to first dc, finish off: 14 dc **each** side.

ASSEMBLY
With Green and working through both loops, whipstitch Squares together *(Fig. 26b, page 126)*, forming 9 vertical strips of 12 Squares each, beginning in ch-1 sp of first corner and ending in ch-1 sp of next corner; whipstitch strips together in same manner.

EDGING
With **right** side facing, join Dk Green with slip st in any corner ch-1 sp; ch 2, (hdc, ch 1, 2 hdc) in same sp, ch 2, † skip next dc, (sc in next dc, ch 2) 12 times, skip next dc, (sc in corner ch-1 sp, ch 2) twice †, repeat from † to † across to last Square, skip next dc, (sc in next dc, ch 2) 11 times, skip next dc, sc in next dc, ch 2, ★ (2 hdc, ch 1, 2 hdc) in next corner ch-1 sp, ch 2, repeat from † to † across to last Square, skip next dc, (sc in next dc, ch 2) 11 times, skip next dc, sc in next dc, ch 2; repeat from ★ around; join with slip st to top of beginning ch-2, finish off.

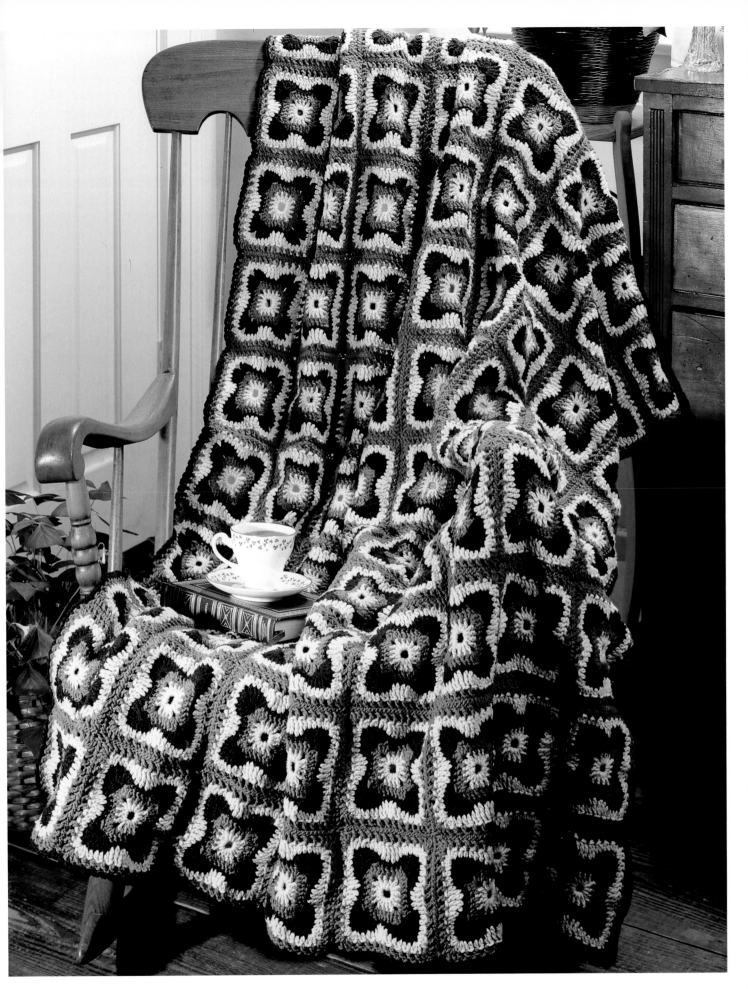

EASTER BLOSSOMS

Stitched in spring colors, this Granny Square afghan reminds me of my Nana's dogwood tree. When its splendid blossoms appeared, we knew Easter was just around the corner.

GRANNY'S DOGWOOD

Finished Size: 48" x 66"

MATERIALS
Worsted Weight Yarn:
    Rose - 18 ounces, (510 grams, 1,235 yards)
    Off-White - 14 ounces, (400 grams, 960 yards)
    Green - 11 ounces, (310 grams, 755 yards)
Crochet hook, size J (6.00 mm) **or** size needed for gauge
Yarn needle

GAUGE SWATCH: Each Square = 9"
Work same as Square.

STITCH GUIDE

TR CLUSTER
★ YO twice, insert hook in ring, YO and pull up a loop, (YO and draw through 2 loops on hook) twice; repeat from ★ 2 times **more**, YO and draw through all 4 loops on hook (*Figs. 16a & b, page 124*).

BEGINNING DC CLUSTER
Ch 2, ★ YO, insert hook in same sp, YO and pull up a loop, YO and draw through 2 loops on hook; repeat from ★ once **more**, YO and draw through all 3 loops on hook.

DC CLUSTER
★ YO, insert hook in sp indicated, YO and pull up a loop, YO and draw through 2 loops on hook; repeat from ★ 2 times **more**, YO and draw through all 4 loops on hook.

SQUARE (Make 35)

With Rose, ch 6; join with slip st to form a ring.

Rnd 1 (Right side): Ch 3, ★ YO twice, insert hook in ring, YO and pull up a loop, (YO and draw through 2 loops on hook) twice; repeat from ★ once **more**, YO and draw through all 3 loops on hook, ch 3, (work tr Cluster, ch 3) 7 times; join with slip st to top of beginning tr Cluster, finish off: 8 Clusters and 8 ch-3 sps.

Note: Loop a short piece of yarn around any stitch to mark Rnd 1 as **right** side.

Rnd 2: With **right** side facing, join Off-White with slip st in any ch-3 sp; work (beginning dc Cluster, ch 3, dc Cluster) in same sp (corner), ch 3, hdc in next ch-3 sp, ch 3, ★ work (dc Cluster, ch 3, dc Cluster) in next ch-3 sp, ch 3, hdc in next ch-3 sp, ch 3; repeat from ★ around; join with slip st to top of beginning dc Cluster, finish off: 8 Clusters and 12 ch-3 sps.

Rnd 3: With **right** side facing, join Green with slip st in any corner ch-3 sp; work (beginning dc Cluster, ch 3, dc Cluster) in same sp, ch 3, (work dc Cluster in next ch-3 sp, ch 3) twice, ★ work (dc Cluster, ch 3, dc Cluster) in next corner ch-3 sp, ch 3, (work dc Cluster in next ch-3 sp, ch 3) twice; repeat from ★ around; join with slip st to top of beginning dc Cluster, finish off: 16 Clusters and 16 ch-3 sps.

Rnd 4: With **right** side facing, join Rose with slip st in any corner ch-3 sp; ch 1, 7 sc in same sp, 4 sc in each of next 3 ch-3 sps, ★ 7 sc in next corner ch-3 sp, 4 sc in each of next 3 ch-3 sps; repeat from ★ around; join with slip st to first sc, finish off: 76 sc.

Rnd 5: With **right** side facing, join Off-White with slip st in center sc of any corner 7-sc group; ch 1, sc in same st, ch 3, (skip next 2 sc, sc in next 2 sc, ch 3) 4 times, skip next 2 sc, ★ sc in next sc, ch 3, (skip next 2 sc, sc in next 2 sc, ch 3) 4 times, skip next 2 sc; repeat from ★ around; join with slip st to first sc: 36 sc.

Rnd 6: Slip st in first ch-3 sp, ch 1, (sc, 3 hdc, sc) in same sp and in next 4 ch-3 sps, ch 1, ★ (sc, 3 hdc, sc) in next 5 ch-3 sps, ch 1; repeat from ★ around; join with slip st to first sc, finish off: 60 hdc.

Rnd 7: With **right** side facing, join Green with slip st in any corner ch-1 sp; ch 3, 4 dc in same sp, ★ † skip next 2 sts, (hdc, sc, hdc) in next hdc, [skip next 4 sts, (hdc, sc, hdc) in next hdc] 4 times, skip next 2 sts †, 5 dc in next corner ch-1 sp; repeat from ★ 2 times **more**, then repeat from † to † once; join with slip st to top of beginning ch-3, finish off: 80 sts.

Rnd 8: With **right** side facing, skip first 2 sts and join Rose with slip st in next dc; ch 2 (**counts as first hdc, now and throughout**), 2 hdc in same st, ★ sc in next st and in each st across to center dc of next corner 5-dc group, 3 hdc in next dc; repeat from ★ 2 times **more**, sc in next st and in each st across; join with slip st to first hdc; do **not** finish off: 88 sts.

Instructions continued on page 120.

ALL-AMERICAN

On Memorial Day — or any patriotic occasion — this all-American wrap makes a wonderful remembrance for a veteran or a member of the armed forces.

PATRIOTIC COLORS

Finished Size: 45" x 59"

MATERIALS
Worsted Weight Yarn:
Blue - 13 ounces, (370 grams, 735 yards)
Dk Blue - 11 ounces, (310 grams, 620 yards)
Burgundy - 11 ounces, (310 grams, 620 yards)
Ecru - 11 ounces, (310 grams, 620 yards)
Crochet hook, size I (5.50 mm) **or** size needed for gauge

GAUGE: In pattern, 14 sc = 4";
12 rows = 3¾"

Gauge Swatch: 4½"w x 4"h
With Blue, ch 17 **loosely**.
Work same as Afghan Body for 13 rows.
Finish off.

STITCH GUIDE

LONG DOUBLE CROCHET (*abbreviated LDC*)
Working around ch-2 of previous 2 rows, YO, insert hook in sc indicated, YO and pull up a loop even with last dc made, (YO and draw through 2 loops on hook) twice **(counts as one dc)** (*Fig. 1*).

Fig. 1

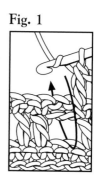

LONG SINGLE CROCHET (*abbreviated LSC*)
Working around ch-2 of previous 2 rows, insert hook in sc indicated, YO and pull up a loop even with last sc made, YO and draw through both loops on hook **(counts as one sc)**.

REVERSE SINGLE CROCHET
(*abbreviated reverse sc*)
Working from **left** to **right**, insert hook in sc to right of hook, YO and draw through, under, and to left of loop on hook (2 loops on hook), YO and draw through both loops on hook (*Figs. 19a-d, page 125*).

AFGHAN BODY

With Blue, ch 155 **loosely**.

Row 1: Sc in second ch from hook and in each ch across changing to Dk Blue in last sc (*Fig. 22a, page 125*): 154 sc.

Row 2 (Right side): Ch 5 **(counts as first dc plus ch 2, now and throughout)**, turn; ★ skip next 2 sc, dc in next 4 sc, ch 2; repeat from ★ across to last 3 sc, skip next 2 sc, dc in last sc: 102 dc and 26 ch-2 sps.
Note: Loop a short piece of yarn around any stitch to mark Row 2 as **right** side.

Row 3: Ch 1, turn; sc in first dc, ch 2, skip next ch-2 sp, ★ sc in next 4 dc, ch 2, skip next ch-2 sp; repeat from ★ across to last dc, sc in last dc changing to Burgundy.

Instructions continued on page 120.

CHRISTMAS

One holiday tradition I always look forward to is stitching fun gifts for my children. A colorful afghan warms Nicholas' room with merry style, and a jolly crocheted elf becomes a cuddly pal for Giovanna.

FESTIVE STRIPES

Finished Size: 49" x 65"

MATERIALS
Worsted Weight Yarn:
    White - 25 ounces, (710 grams, 1,645 yards)
    Red - 12 ounces, (340 grams, 790 yards)
    Green - 11 ounces, (310 grams, 725 yards)
Crochet hook, size I (5.50 mm) **or** size needed for gauge

Note: Each row is worked across length of Afghan.
    When joining yarn and finishing off, leave a 7" end
    to be worked into fringe.

GAUGE: In pattern, 14 sts = 4"

Gauge Swatch: 5³/₄" wide
Ch 21 **loosely.**
Work same as Afghan for 5 rows: 20 sts.
Finish off.

COLOR SEQUENCE
2 Rows **each** Red **(Fig. 22a, page 125),** ★ White, Green, White, Red; repeat from ★ throughout.

AFGHAN
With Red, ch 229 **loosely.**
Row 1 (Right side): Sc in second ch from hook and in next 3 chs, (dc in next 4 chs, sc in next 4 chs) across: 228 sts.
Note: Loop a short piece of yarn around any stitch to mark Row 1 as **right** side.
Row 2: Ch 1, turn; sc in first 4 sc, (dc in next 4 dc, sc in next 4 sc) across.
Row 3: Ch 3 **(counts as first dc, now and throughout),** turn; dc in next 3 sc, (sc in next 4 dc, dc in next 4 sc) across.
Row 4: Ch 3, turn; dc in next 3 dc, (sc in next 4 sc, dc in next 4 dc) across.
Row 5: Ch 1, turn; sc in first 4 dc, (dc in next 4 sc, sc in next 4 dc) across.
Repeat Rows 2-5 until Afghan measures approximately 49" from beginning ch, ending by working Row 2 with Red. Finish off.

Holding 2 or 3 strands of corresponding color together, add additional fringe to each stripe across short edges of Afghan **(Figs. 27a & b, page 126).**

ENCHANTING ELF

Finished Size: 5¹/₂" high (including Cap)

MATERIALS
Sport Weight Yarn:
    Pink - 25 yards
    Elf clothes
        Red - 15 yards
        White - 18 yards
        Green - 3 yards
Brushed Acrylic Worsted Weight Yarn: White - 3 yards
Crochet hook, size D (3.25 mm) **or** size needed for gauge
Tapestry, yarn, and soft sculpture needles
Black embroidery floss
Polyester fiberfill
Jingle bell

GAUGE: 6 dc and 3 rows = 1"

Gauge Swatch: ³/₄" diameter
Work same as Elf Head for 2 rnds.

Instructions continued on page 96.

STITCH GUIDE

PICOT
Ch 3, slip st in third ch from hook.

DECREASE
Pull up a loop in next 2 sts, YO and draw through all 3 loops on hook.

ELF
HEAD AND BODY

Rnd 1 (Right side): With Pink, ch 2, 8 sc in second ch from hook; do **not** join, place marker.

*Note: Do **not** join at end of rounds. Using a 2" scrap piece of yarn, place marker at beginning of rounds, moving after each round is complete.*

Rnd 2: 2 Sc in each sc around: 16 sc.

Rnd 3: (Sc in next sc, 2 sc in next sc) around: 24 sc.

Rnds 4-8: Sc in each sc around.

Rnd 9: (Skip next sc, sc in next 2 sc) around: 16 sc.
Stuff Head firmly with polyester fiberfill.

Rnd 10: (Skip next sc, sc in next sc) around: 8 sc.

Rnds 11 and 12: Sc in each sc around.

Rnd 13: 2 Sc in each sc around: 16 sc.

Rnds 14-21: Sc in each sc around.

Rnd 22: (Skip next sc, sc in next sc) around: 8 sc.
Stuff Body firmly with polyester fiberfill.

Rnd 23: (Skip next sc, sc in next sc) around; slip st in next sc, finish off: 4 sc.

ARM (Make 2)

Rnd 1 (Right side): With Pink, ch 2, 6 sc in second ch from hook; do **not** join, place marker.

Rnds 2-8: Sc in each sc around.

Rnd 9 (Hand and Fingers): Sc in next 3 sc, skip next 2 sc, slip st from **wrong** side in next sc, work Picot 4 times; working in chs at base of each Picot, skip first Picot, pull up a loop in each of next 3 Picots, insert hook from **wrong** side in last sc worked, YO and draw through st and all 4 loops on hook, work Picot, slip st from **wrong** side in next sc; finish off.

LEG (Make 2)

Rnd 1 (Right side): With Pink, ch 2, 9 sc in second ch from hook; do **not** join, place marker.

Rnds 2-9: Sc in each sc around.
Stuff Leg lightly with polyester fiberfill.

Rnd 10: (Skip next sc, sc in next 2 sc) around: 6 sc.

Rnd 11: Sc in each sc around.

Rnd 12: 2 Dc in each of next 3 sc, sc in next 3 sc: 9 sts.

Rnd 13: Working in Back Loops Only (*Fig. 20, page 125*), sc in next dc, decrease 3 times, stuff lightly with polyester fiberfill, decrease; slip st in next sc, finish off leaving a long end for sewing: 5 sts.
Thread tapestry needle with end and weave through remaining sts; gather tightly and secure.

ASSEMBLY

Thread a soft sculpture needle with a doubled 24" length of Pink. Insert needle through Arm (*Fig. 1*) between Rnds 1 and 2 (at 1), then back into Arm one stitch over (at 2) and through Arm again (at 1). Insert needle completely through upper Body between Rnds 14 and 15 and out second side (at 3), through second Arm between Rnds 1 and 2, then back into Arm one stitch over (at 4), through Arm again (at 3), and back through upper Body (at 5).

Pull both ends of yarn so that the Arms fit tightly against the upper Body, but are still able to move freely at sides. Knot the strands tightly, weave the ends under several stitches, and cut close to work.

Attach Legs in same manner, inserting needle between Rnds 1 and 2 on Legs and between Rnds 21 and 22 on Body.

Fig. 1

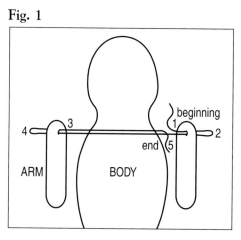

Using 6 strands of black embroidery floss, add French knot eyes allowing needle to pass between Rnds 5 and 6, and leaving 4 sts between eyes (*Fig. 32, page 127*).

RIGHT EAR

With top of Head toward you and face up, join Pink with slip st on Rnd 5 in fourth st to the **right** of the eye; ch 3, slip st in second ch from hook and in next ch, sc in same st as joining, sc in next st on Rnd 6, slip st in next st on Rnd 7; finish off.

LEFT EAR

With Legs toward you and face up, join Pink with slip st on Rnd 7 in fourth st to the **right** of the eye; sc in next st on Rnd 6, sc in next st on Rnd 5, ch 4, slip st in second ch from hook and in next ch, skip last ch, slip st in same st as last sc; finish off.

MUSTACHE

With Brushed Acrylic yarn, ch 8; finish off.
Trim ends just above knot.
Sew center of Mustache to Head, between Rnds 6 and 7.

BEARD AND HAIR

With 2 strands of Brushed Acrylic yarn and yarn needle, work Turkey Loop St for Beard and Hair as follows using photo as a guide for placement: Bring needle up through a st and back down through same st (point A), forming a loop on **right** side of work. Bring needle up to either side of loop (point B) and back down through point A, locking st. Begin next st at point B **(Fig. 2)**.

Fig. 2

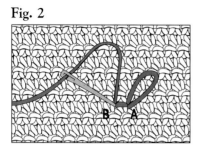

CLOTHES

Note: Use Sport Weight yarn throughout.

SUIT

With White, ch 17 **loosely**.

Row 1 (Right side): Sc in second ch from hook and in each ch across: 16 sc.

Note: Loop a short piece of yarn around any stitch to mark Row 1 as **right** side.

Row 2: Ch 1, turn; 2 sc in each sc across changing to Red in last sc worked **(Fig. 22a, page 125)**: 32 sc.

Row 3: Ch 1, turn; sc in Back Loop Only of each sc across.

Row 4: Ch 1, turn; working in both loops, sc in first 4 sc, ch 4 **loosely**, skip next 9 sc (armhole), sc in next 6 sc, ch 4 **loosely**, skip next 9 sc (armhole), sc in last 4 sc: 14 sc.

Row 5: Ch 3 **(counts as first dc, now and throughout),** turn; dc in next 2 sc, 2 dc in next sc, dc in next 4 chs, 2 dc in next sc, dc in next 4 sc, 2 dc in next sc, dc in next 4 chs, 2 dc in next sc, dc in last 3 sc: 26 dc.

Row 6: Ch 1, turn; sc in each dc across.

Note: Begin working in rounds.

Rnd 1: Ch 3, turn; dc in next 3 sc, 2 dc in next sc, (dc in next 5 sc, 2 dc in next sc) 3 times, dc in last 3 sc; join with slip st to first dc: 30 dc.

Rnd 2: Ch 3, do **not** turn; dc in next dc and in each dc around; join with slip st to first dc, do **not** finish off.

LEFT LEG

Rnd 1: Ch 3, skip next 14 dc, (slip st, ch 2, dc) in next dc, dc in next 14 dc, dc in next 3 chs; skip ch-2 and join with slip st to first dc: 18 dc.

Rnd 2: Ch 3, dc in next dc and in each dc around; join with slip st to first dc changing to White.

Rnd 3: Ch 1, sc in Back Loop Only of each dc around; join with slip st to first sc.

Rnd 4: Slip st in Back Loop Only of each sc around; finish off.

RIGHT LEG

Rnd 1: With **right** side facing, join Red with slip st in top of beginning ch-3 on Rnd 2 of Suit; ch 2, dc in same st and in next 14 dc, dc in free loop of next 3 chs; skip ch-2 and join with slip st to first dc: 18 dc.

Rnds 2-4: Repeat Rnds 2-4 of Left Leg.

SLEEVE

Rnd 1: With **right** side facing and working in free loops of ch-4 and in unworked sc of armhole, join White with slip st in first ch; ch 1, sc in same st and in next 3 chs, hdc in side of next sc, dc in Back Loop Only of next 9 sc, hdc in side of next sc; join with slip st to first sc: 15 sts.

Rnds 2 and 3: Ch 1, sc in first 4 sc, hdc in next hdc, dc in next 9 dc, hdc in next hdc; join with slip st to first sc.

Rnd 4: Ch 1, sc in each st around; join with slip st to first sc.

Rnd 5: Slip st in Back Loop Only of each sc around; finish off.

Repeat for second Sleeve.

TIES

With White, ch 30; with **right** side facing, sc in free loop of each beginning ch across neck edge **(Fig. 21b, page 125)**; ch 30; finish off.

CAP

Rnd 1 (Right side): With Red, ch 4, 5 dc in fourth ch from hook; join with slip st to top of beginning ch changing to White **(Fig. 22b, page 125)**: 6 sts.

Rnd 2: Ch 3, dc in same st, 2 dc in each of next 5 dc; join with slip st to first dc changing to Green: 12 dc.

Rnd 3: Ch 3, 2 dc in next dc, (dc in next dc, 2 dc in next dc) around; join with slip st to first dc changing to Red: 18 dc.

Rnd 4: Ch 3, dc in next dc, 2 dc in next dc, (dc in next 2 dc, 2 dc in next dc) around; join with slip st to first dc changing to White: 24 dc.

Rnd 5: Ch 3, dc in next 2 dc, 2 dc in next dc, (dc in next 3 dc, 2 dc in next dc) around; join with slip st to first dc changing to Green: 30 dc.

Rnd 6: Ch 1, sc in Back Loop Only of each dc around; join with slip st to first sc.

Rnd 7: Ch 1, sc in both loops of each sc around; join with slip st to first sc, finish off.

Sew jingle bell to top of Cap. Tack Cap to top of Head if desired.

A FAMILY NOEL

*Even if the weather doesn't
promise a white Christmas, a
dear family will be thrilled with the
arrival of this crocheted snowfall!
Bits of holiday red and green
enhance the lacy snowflakes.*

CHRISTMAS SNOWFLAKES

Finished Size: 45" x 59"

MATERIALS
Worsted Weight Yarn:
    White - 22 ounces, (620 grams, 1,445 yards)
    Red - 9 ounces, (260 grams, 590 yards)
    Green - 7 ounces, (200 grams, 460 yards)
Crochet hook, size G (4.00 mm) **or** size needed for gauge
Yarn needle

GAUGE SWATCH: 4¹/₂" (straight edge to straight edge)
Work same as Motif A.

STITCH GUIDE

DECREASE (uses next 2 dc)
★ YO, insert hook in **next** dc, YO and pull up a loop, YO and draw through 2 loops on hook; repeat from ★ once **more**, YO and draw through all 3 loops on hook **(counts as one dc)**.

FRONT POST TREBLE CROCHET
  (abbreviated FPtr)
YO twice, insert hook from **front** to **back** around post of st on Rnd 1 **below** next dc, YO and pull up a loop **(Fig. 12, page 124)**, (YO and draw through 2 loops on hook) 3 times. Skip dc behind FPtr.

MOTIF A (Make 78)
Rnd 1 (Right side)**:** With White, ch 4, 11 dc in fourth ch from hook; join with slip st to top of beginning ch, finish off: 12 sts.
Note: Loop a short piece of yarn around any stitch to mark Rnd 1 as **right** side.
Rnd 2: With **right** side facing, join Red with slip st in same st as joining; ch 3 **(counts as first dc, now and throughout)**, dc in same st, 2 dc in next dc, ch 1, (2 dc in each of next 2 dc, ch 1) around; join with slip st to first dc: 24 dc.
Rnd 3: Ch 3, dc in same st, decrease, 2 dc in next dc, ch 2, ★ 2 dc in next dc, decrease, 2 dc in next dc, ch 2; repeat from ★ around; join with slip st to first dc, finish off: 30 dc.
Rnd 4: With **right** side facing, join White with slip st in same st as joining; ch 3, dc in same st and in next dc, work FPtr, dc in next dc, 2 dc in next dc, ch 2, ★ 2 dc in next dc, dc in next dc, work FPtr, dc in next dc, 2 dc in next dc, ch 2; repeat from ★ around; join with slip st to first dc, finish off: 42 sts and 6 ch-2 sps.

MOTIF B (Make 60)
Rnd 1 (Right side)**:** With White, ch 4, 11 dc in fourth ch from hook; join with slip st to top of beginning ch, finish off: 12 sts.
Note: Mark Rnd 1 as **right** side.
Rnd 2: With **right** side facing, join Green with slip st in same st as joining; ch 3, dc in same st, 2 dc in next dc, ch 1, (2 dc in each of next 2 dc, ch 1) around; join with slip st to first dc: 24 dc.
Rnds 3 and 4: Work same as Motif A: 42 sts and 6 ch-2 sps.

ASSEMBLY
With White, using Placement Diagram, page 120, as a guide, and working through both loops, whipstitch Motifs together **(Fig. 26b, page 126)**, forming 6 vertical strips of 13 Motifs each (A) and 5 vertical strips of 12 Motifs each (B), beginning in second ch of first corner ch-2 and ending in first ch of next corner ch-2; whipstitch strips together in same manner.

EDGING
With **right** side facing, join White with slip st in any dc; ch 1, sc evenly around working 2 sc in each corner ch-2 sp; join with slip st to first sc, finish off.

BORDER

Note: Work into Rings with **right** side of each Ring facing you at all times.

Rnd 1: Holding First and Second Rings together, with remaining Rings to the right, and working through **both** Rings, join Off-White with sc in any ch-3 sp *(see Joining With Sc, page 125)*, ch 3; working through one Ring only, (sc in next ch-3 sp, ch 3) 9 times, skip next 3 ch-3 sps on next Ring, sc in next ch-3 sp on **both** Rings, ch 3; ★ working through one Ring only, (sc in next ch-3 sp, ch 3) twice; working through **both** Rings, sc in next ch-3 sp on same Ring **and** any ch-3 sp of next Ring, ch 3; repeat from ★ 24 times **more**; working through one Ring only, (sc in next ch-3 sp, ch 3) 9 times, † skip next 3 ch-3 sps on next Ring, sc in next ch-3 sp on **both** Rings, ch 3, working through one Ring only, (sc in next ch-3 sp, ch 3) twice †, repeat from † to † across; join with slip st to first sc: 170 ch-3 sps.

Rnd 2: Slip st in first ch-3 sp, ch 1, 2 sc in same sp and in each of next 2 ch-3 sps, 4 sc in each of next 4 ch-3 sps, 2 sc in each of next 81 ch-3 sps, 4 sc in each of next 4 ch-3 sps, 2 sc in each ch-3 sp across; join with slip st to first sc, finish off: 356 sc.

Rnd 3: With **right** side facing, join Green with slip st in same st as joining; ch 2, (YO, insert hook in same st, YO and pull up a loop even with loop on hook) twice, YO and draw through all 5 loops on hook **(first Puff St made)**, (ch 1, skip next sc, work Puff St in next sc) 4 times, (ch 2, skip next sc, work Puff St in next sc) 7 times, (ch 1, skip next sc, work Puff St in next sc) 82 times, (ch 2, skip next sc, work Puff St in next sc) 7 times, ch 1, skip next sc, (work Puff St in next sc, ch 1, skip next sc) across; join with slip st to first Puff St: 178 Puff Sts and 178 sps.

Rnd 4: Ch 1, sc in same st, (sc in next ch-1 sp and in next Puff St) 4 times, place marker around last sc made for joining placement, (2 sc in next ch-2 sp, sc in next Puff St) 7 times, place marker around last sc made for joining placement, (sc in next ch-1 sp and in next Puff St) 82 times, place marker around last sc made for joining placement, (2 sc in next ch-2 sp, sc in next Puff St) 7 times, place marker around last sc made for joining placement, sc in next ch-1 sp, (sc in next Puff St and in next ch-1 sp) across; join with slip st to first sc, finish off.

ASSEMBLY

Place two Strips with **wrong** sides together and bottom edges at the same end. With Green and working through inside loops only, whipstitch Strips together *(Fig. 26a, page 126)*, beginning in first marked sc and ending in next marked sc.

EDGING

Rnd 1: With **right** side facing, join Green with sc in marked sc at top right edge, remove marker; † sc in next 3 sc, 2 sc in next sc, (sc in next 5 sc, 2 sc in next sc) twice, ★ sc in next 4 sc, skip joining, sc in next 3 sc, 2 sc in next sc, (sc in next 5 sc, 2 sc in next sc) twice; repeat from ★ 6 times **more** †, sc in each sc across to second marked sc, sc in marked sc, remove all markers, repeat from † to † once, sc in each sc across; join with slip st to first sc.

Rnd 2: Ch 1; work reverse sc in each sc around; join with slip st to first st, finish off.

Valentine's Day (continued from page 6)

TWO SIDE JOINING

Rnd 5 (Joining rnd): Slip st in first ch-5 sp, ch 1, sc in same sp, ch 5, sc in next ch-5 sp, ch 5, (sc, ch 7, sc) in next corner ch-3 sp, (ch 5, sc in next sp) 4 times, ch 3, with **wrong** sides together, sc in corresponding corner ch-7 sp on **previous Motif**, ch 3, sc in same sp on **new Motif**, ★ (ch 2, sc in next ch-5 sp on **previous Motif**, ch 2, sc in next ch-5 sp on **new Motif**) 4 times, ch 3, sc in corresponding corner ch-7 sp on **previous Motif**, ch 3, sc in same sp on **new Motif**; repeat from ★ once **more**, ch 5, sc in next ch-5 sp, ch 5; join with slip st to first sc, finish off.

FIRST HEART
CENTER

Foundation: Ch 4, work 2-dc Cluster in forth ch from hook, working in top 3 loops of Clusters *(Fig. 1)*, (ch 3, work 2-dc Cluster in top of Cluster just worked) 5 times.

Fig. 1

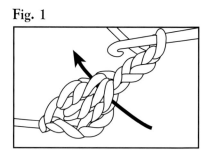

Rnd 1: Ch 4, working in top 3 loops of Clusters, (work 3-dc Cluster, ch 4) twice in next Cluster, ★ sc in next Cluster, ch 4, (work 3-dc Cluster, ch 4) twice in next Cluster; repeat from ★ once **more**, slip st in bottom of same Cluster, ch 4; working in same sps on second side of Foundation, work 3-dc Cluster in next sp, (skip next sp, work 3-dc Cluster in next sp) twice, ch 4; join with slip st to first ch, do **not** finish off.

EDGING

Rnd 1 (Right side): Slip st in first ch-4 sp, ch 1, 7 sc in same sp, 3 sc in each of next 3 ch-4 sps, 5 sc in next ch-4 sp, 3 sc in each of next 3 ch-4 sps, 7 sc in next ch-4 sp, 5 sc in next ch-4 sp, skip next Cluster, sc in next Cluster, 5 sc in last ch-4 sp; join with slip st to first sc: 48 sc.

Note: Mark Rnd 1 as **right** side.

Rnd 2: Ch 1, sc in first 18 sc, 3 sc in next sc, sc in each sc across; join with slip st to first sc: 50 sc.

Rnd 3: Working in sps between sts *(Fig. 23, page 125)*, hold yarn at back of work, insert hook from **front** to **back** between first 2 sts, YO and pull up a loop, ★ insert hook in next sp, YO and draw through loop on hook; repeat from ★ around; join with slip st to first st.

Rnd 4: Working on Rnd 2, slip st in next sc, ch 1, sc in same st, ch 3, (skip next sc, sc in next sc, ch 3) 8 times, skip next sc, (sc, ch 3) twice in next sc, (skip next sc, sc in next sc, ch 3) 10 times, skip next sc, decrease, skip next 3 sc, decrease, ch 3, skip next sc, sc in next sc, ch 3, skip last sc; join with slip st to first sc, finish off.

NEXT 29 HEARTS

Work same as First Heart through Rnd 3 of Edging. Work Joining to form 2 strips of 6 Hearts each and 2 strips of 9 Hearts each.

JOINING

Rnd 4 (Joining rnd): Working on Rnd 2, slip st in next sc, ch 1, sc in same st, ch 3, (skip next sc, sc in next sc, ch 3) 8 times, skip next sc, (sc, ch 3, sc) in next sc, (ch 3, skip next sc, sc in next sc) 5 times, ch 1, with **wrong** sides together, skip 5 ch-3 sps from point on **previous Heart** and sc in next ch-3 sp, ch 1, ★ skip next sc on **new Heart**, sc in next sc, ch 1, sc in next ch-3 sp on **previous Heart**, ch 1; repeat from ★ once **more**, (skip next sc on **new Heart**, sc in next sc, ch 3) 3 times, skip next sc, decrease, skip next 3 sc, decrease, ch 3, skip next sc, sc in next sc, ch 3, skip last sc; join with slip st to first sc, finish off.

JOINING STRIPS

Note: Hearts are joined to Motifs along top 6 loops at each Heart. Match strips to corresponding edge of Afghan.

With **right** side of Afghan facing, join yarn with slip st in any corner ch-7 sp; ch 1, ★ (sc, ch 3) twice in same corner sp on **Motif**, with **wrong** sides together, sc in first ch-3 sp on top of **First Heart** of strip, ch 3, (sc in next ch-5 sp on **Motif**, ch 3, sc in next ch-3 sp on **Heart**, ch 3) 4 times, sc in next corner loop on **Motif**, ch 3, sc in next ch-3 sp on **Heart**, ch 3, † (sc, ch 3) twice in next joining sc between **Motifs**, sc in first ch-3 sp on next **Heart**, ch 3, skip next corner loop, (sc in next ch-5 sp on **Motif**, ch 3, sc in next ch-3 sp on **Heart**, ch 3) 4 times, sc in next corner loop on **Motif**, ch 3, sc in next ch-3 sp on **Heart**, ch 3 †, repeat from † to † across; repeat from ★ around; join with slip st to first sc, finish off.

CORNER HEART

Work same as first Heart through Rnd 3 of Edging.

Rnd 4 (Joining rnd): Working on Rnd 2, slip st in next sc, ch 1, sc in same st, (ch 3, skip next sc, sc in next sc) 4 times, ch 1, with **wrong** sides together, skip 5 ch-3 sps from point on **previous Heart** and sc in next ch-3 sp, ch 1, † skip next sc on **corner Heart**, sc in next sc, ch 1, sc in next ch-3 sp on **previous Heart**, ch 1 †, repeat from † to † once **more**, (skip next sc on **corner Heart**, sc in next sc, ch 3) twice, skip next sc, sc in next sc, ch 1, sc in corner on-3 sp on corner **Motif**, ch 1, sc in same st on **corner Heart**, (ch 3, skip next sc, sc in next sc) twice, ch 1, sc in corresponding ch-3 sp on **previous Heart**, ch 1, repeat from † to † twice, (skip next sc on **corner Heart**, sc in next sc, ch 3) 6 times, skip next sc, decrease, skip next 3 sc, decrease, ch 3, skip next sc, sc in next sc, ch 3, skip last sc; join with slip st to first sc, finish off. Repeat for remaining 3 corners.

Welcome, Neighbor! (continued from page 8)

Row 9: Ch 4, turn; dc in next dc, ch 1, ★ dc in next 5 dc, 2 dc in next dc, ch 3, skip next ch-3 sp, (sc in next ch-3 sp, ch 3) 7 times, skip next ch-3 sp, 2 dc in next dc, dc in next 5 dc, ch 1, dc in next dc, ch 1; repeat from ★ across to last dc, dc in last dc: 93 dc and 62 sps.

Row 10: Ch 4, turn; dc in next dc, ch 1, ★ dc in next 6 dc, 2 dc in next dc, ch 3, skip next ch-3 sp, (sc in next ch-3 sp, ch 3) 6 times, skip next ch-3 sp, 2 dc in next dc, dc in next 6 dc, ch 1, dc in next dc, ch 1; repeat from ★ across to last dc, dc in last dc: 105 dc and 56 sps.

Row 11: Ch 4, turn; dc in next dc, ch 1, ★ dc in next 7 dc, 2 dc in next dc, ch 3, skip next ch-3 sp, (sc in next ch-3 sp, ch 3) 5 times, skip next ch-3 sp, 2 dc in next dc, dc in next 7 dc, ch 1, dc in next dc, ch 1; repeat from ★ across to last dc, dc in last dc: 117 dc and 50 sps.

Row 12: Ch 4, turn; dc in next dc, ch 1, ★ dc in next 8 dc, 2 dc in next dc, ch 3, skip next ch-3 sp, (sc in next ch-3 sp, ch 3) 4 times, skip next ch-3 sp, 2 dc in next dc, dc in next 8 dc, ch 1, dc in next dc, ch 1; repeat from ★ across to last dc, dc in last dc: 129 dc and 44 sps.

Row 13: Ch 4, turn; dc in next dc, ch 1, ★ dc in next 9 dc, 2 dc in next dc, ch 3, skip next ch-3 sp, (sc in next ch-3 sp, ch 3) 3 times, skip next ch-3 sp, 2 dc in next dc, dc in next 9 dc, ch 1, dc in next dc, ch 1; repeat from ★ across to last dc, dc in last dc: 141 dc and 38 sps.

Row 14: Ch 4, turn; dc in next dc, ch 1, ★ dc in next 10 dc, 2 dc in next dc, ch 3, skip next ch-3 sp, (sc in next ch-3 sp, ch 3) twice, skip next ch-3 sp, 2 dc in next dc, dc in next 10 dc, ch 1, dc in next dc, ch 1; repeat from ★ across to last dc, dc in last dc; do **not** finish off: 153 dc and 32 sps.

Instructions continued on page 102.

Welcome, Neighbor! *(continued from page 101)*

Row 15: Ch 4, turn; dc in next dc, ch 1, ★ dc in next 11 dc, 2 dc in next dc, ch 3, skip next ch-3 sp, sc in next ch-3 sp, ch 3, skip next ch-3 sp, 2 dc in next dc, dc in next 11 dc, ch 1, dc in next dc, ch 1; repeat from ★ across to last dc, dc in last dc: 165 dc and 26 sps.

Row 16: Ch 4, turn; dc in next dc, ch 1, ★ dc in next 12 dc, 2 dc in next dc, ch 3, skip next 2 ch-3 sps, 2 dc in next dc, dc in next 12 dc, ch 1, dc in next dc, ch 1; repeat from ★ across to last dc, dc in last dc: 177 dc and 20 sps.

Row 17: Ch 4, turn; dc in next dc, ch 1, ★ dc in next 14 dc, 3 dc in next ch-3 sp, dc in next 14 dc, ch 1, dc in next dc, ch 1; repeat from ★ across to last dc, dc in last dc: 195 dc and 14 ch-1 sps.

Rows 18 and 19: Ch 4, turn; dc in next dc, ch 1, ★ dc in each dc across to next ch-1 sp, ch 1, dc in next dc, ch 1; repeat from ★ across to last dc, dc in last dc.

Row 20: Ch 4, turn; dc in next dc, ch 1, dc in next dc, ★ (ch 1, skip next dc, dc in next dc) 15 times, (ch 1, dc in next dc) twice; repeat from ★ across; finish off.

ASSEMBLY

Holding two Panels together, matching markers, and working through both loops, whipstitch Panels together to form half of Afghan *(Fig. 26b, page 126)*, beginning in marked ch and ending in last ch.
Whipstitch remaining two Panels together in same manner.
Holding halves together with markers to the right and working through both loops of sts across Row 20, whipstitch halves together, beginning in first dc and ending in last dc.

EDGING

Working from **left** to **right** across either long edge, join yarn with slip st in first dc at left corner; ch 1, work reverse sc in each dc and in each ch across; finish off.
With same side facing, repeat across remaining long edge.

Holding 3 strands of yarn together, add fringe to every other row across short edges of Afghan *(Figs. 27a & b, page 126)*.

If Friends Were Flowers… *(continued from page 10)*

Rnd 11: Slip st in next 2 dc and in sp **before** next dc *(Fig. 23, page 125)*, ch 1, sc in same sp, ch 5, skip next 3 dc, sc in sp **before** next dc, ch 5, ★ † (sc, ch 5) twice in next corner ch-3 sp, skip next 2 dc, sc in sp **before** next dc †, ch 5, (skip next 3 dc, sc in sp **before** next dc, ch 5) across to within 2 dc of next corner ch-3 sp; repeat from ★ 2 times **more**, then repeat from † to † once, (ch 5, skip next 3 dc, sc in sp **before** next dc) across, ch 2, dc in first sc to form last sp: 44 sps.

Rnd 12: Ch 1, sc in same sp, ch 5, ★ (sc in next ch-5 sp, ch 5) across to next corner ch-5 sp, (sc, ch 5) twice in corner ch-5 sp; repeat from ★ 3 times **more**, (sc in next ch-5 sp, ch 5) across; join with slip st to first sc, finish off: 48 ch-5 sps.

ADDITIONAL SQUARES

Work same as First Square through Rnd 11.
Work One Side or Two Side Joining to form 5 vertical strips of 7 Squares each.
Note: When working into corner sp that has been previously joined, work into joining slip st.

ONE SIDE JOINING

Rnd 12 (Joining rnd): Ch 1, sc in same sp, ch 5, (sc in next ch-5 sp, ch 5) twice, ★ (sc, ch 5) twice in next corner ch-5 sp, (sc in next ch-5 sp, ch 5) across to next corner ch-5 sp; repeat from ★ once **more**, sc in corner ch-5 sp, ch 2, with **wrong** sides together, slip st in corner sp on **previous Square** *(Fig. 24, page 126)*, ch 2, sc in same sp on **new Square**, (ch 2, slip st in next ch-5 sp on **previous Square**, ch 2, sc in next ch-5 sp on **new Square**) 11 times, ch 2, slip st in corner sp on **previous Square**, ch 2, sc in same sp on **new Square**, ch 5, (sc in next ch-5 sp, ch 5) across; join with slip st to first sc, finish off.

TWO SIDE JOINING

Rnd 12 (Joining rnd): Ch 1, sc in same sp, (ch 5, sc in next ch-5 sp) twice, (ch 5, sc) twice in next corner ch-5 sp, (ch 5, sc in next ch-5 sp) 11 times, ch 2, with **wrong** sides together, slip st in corner sp on **previous Square**, ch 2, sc in same sp on **new Square**, ★ (ch 2, slip st in next ch-5 sp on **previous Square**, ch 2, sc in next ch-5 sp on **new Square**) 11 times, ch 2, slip st in corresponding corner on **previous Square**, ch 2, sc in same sp on **new Square**; repeat from ★ once **more**, ch 5, (sc in next ch-5 sp, ch 5) across; join with slip st to first sc, finish off.

Birthday Jewels *(continued from page 12)*

Row 4: Ch 2, turn; ★ † work FPdc around each of next 2 dc, (dc in next 2 FPdc, work FPdc around each of next 2 dc) 3 times †, work BPdc around each of next 2 FPdc, work FPdc around next BPdc, work BPdc around each of next 2 FPdc, work FPdc around each of next 6 BPdc, work BPdc around each of next 2 FPdc, work FPdc around next BPdc, work BPdc around each of next 2 FPdc; repeat from ★ across to last 15 sts, then repeat from † to † once, hdc in last hdc.

Row 5: Ch 2, turn; ★ † dc in next 2 FPdc, (work FPdc around each of next 2 dc, dc in next 2 FPdc) 3 times †, work FPdc around each of next 2 BPdc, work BPdc around next FPdc, work FPdc around each of next 2 BPdc, work BPdc around each of next 6 FPdc, work FPdc around each of next 2 BPdc, work BPdc around next FPdc, work FPdc around each of next 2 BPdc; repeat from ★ across to last 15 sts, then repeat from † to † once, hdc in last hdc.

Row 6: Ch 2, turn; ★ † work FPdc around each of next 2 dc, (dc in next 2 FPdc, work FPdc around each of next 2 dc) 3 times †, work BPdc around each of next 2 FPdc, work FPdc around next BPdc, work BPdc around each of next 2 FPdc, skip next 3 BPdc, work FPtr around each of next 3 BPdc, working in **front** of 3 FPtr just made, work FPtr around each of 3 skipped BPdc, work BPdc around each of next 2 FPdc, work FPdc around next BPdc, work BPdc around each of next 2 FPdc; repeat from ★ across to last 15 sts, then repeat from † to † once, hdc in last hdc.
Repeat Rows 3-6 until Afghan Body measures approximately 60" from beginning ch, ending by working Row 4; do **not** finish off.

EDGING

Rnd 1: Ch 1, turn; sc evenly around entire Afghan working 3 sc in each corner; join with slip st to first sc.
Rnd 2: Ch 1, turn; sc in each sc around working 3 sc in each corner sc; join with slip st to first sc, finish off.

Holding 7 strands of yarn together, add fringe evenly across short edges of Afghan (*Figs. 27a & b, page 126*).

You're a "Purr-fect Pal" (continued from page 14)

BORDER

Rnd 1: Ch 1, turn; sc in first sc, ch 1, (sc in next sc, ch 1) across to last sc, (sc, ch 2, sc) in last sc, ch 1; working in end of rows, skip first 2 rows, (sc in next row, ch 1, skip next row) across; working in free loops of beginning ch (*Fig. 21b, page 125*), (sc, ch 2, sc) in first ch, ch 1, (skip next ch, sc in next ch, ch 1) across to last 2 chs, skip next ch, (sc, ch 2, sc) in last ch, ch 1; working in end of rows, skip first row, sc in next row, ch 1, (skip next row, sc in next row, ch 1) across to last 2 rows, skip last 2 rows, sc in same st as first sc, ch 2; join with slip st to first sc, finish off: 56 sc and 56 sps.
Rnd 2: With **wrong** side facing, join Green with sc in same st as joining (*see Joining With Sc, page 125*); ch 3, skip next corner ch-2, sc in next sc, ★ (ch 1, sc in next sc) across to next corner ch-2, ch 3, skip corner ch-2, sc in next sc; repeat from ★ 2 times **more**, ch 1, (sc in next sc, ch 1) across; join with slip st to first sc, finish off.
Rnd 3: With **right** side facing, join Ecru with sc in same st as joining; ★ † (ch 1, sc in next sc) across to next corner ch-3; working **behind** corner ch-3, (dc, ch 3, dc) in corner ch-2 sp on Rnd 1 †, sc in next sc; repeat from ★ 2 times **more**, then repeat from † to † once; join with slip st to first sc: 64 sts and 56 sps.
Rnd 4: Slip st in first ch-1 sp, ch 4 (**counts as first dc plus ch 1, now and throughout**), ★ (dc in next ch-1 sp, ch 1) across to within 2 sts of next corner ch-3 sp, skip next sc, dc in next dc, ch 1, (dc, ch 3, dc) in corner ch-3 sp, ch 1, dc in next dc, ch 1; repeat from ★ around; join with slip st to first dc, finish off.

ASSEMBLY

With Ecru, matching sts of bottom edge of one Square to top edge of next Square, and working through both loops, whipstitch Squares together (*Fig. 26b, page 126*), forming 5 vertical strips of 7 Squares each, beginning in center ch of first corner ch-3 and ending in center ch of next corner ch-3; whipstitch strips together in same manner, keeping bottom edges at same end.

EDGING

Rnd 1: With **wrong** side facing, join Ecru with sc in any corner ch-3 sp; ch 2, sc in same sp, ch 1, (sc in next dc, ch 1) 17 times, [sc in next joining, ch 1, (sc in next dc, ch 1) 17 times] across to next corner ch-3 sp, ★ (sc, ch 2, sc) in corner ch-3 sp, ch 1, (sc in next dc, ch 1) 17 times, [sc in next joining, ch 1, (sc in next dc, ch 1) 17 times] across to next corner ch-3 sp; repeat from ★ 2 times **more**; join with slip st to first sc: 436 sc.
Rnd 2: Ch 4, turn; ★ (dc in next sc, ch 1) across to next corner ch-2 sp, (dc, ch 3, dc) in corner ch-2 sp, ch 1; repeat from ★ around; join with slip st to first dc, finish off: 444 dc.
Rnd 3: With **wrong** side facing, join Green with sc in any corner ch-3 sp; ch 3, sc in same sp, ch 1, skip next dc, (sc in next dc, ch 1) across to within one dc of next corner ch-3 sp, skip next dc, ★ (sc, ch 3, sc) in corner ch-3 sp, ch 1, skip next dc, (sc in next dc, ch 1) across to within one dc of next corner ch-3 sp, skip next dc; repeat from ★ around; join with slip st to first sc, finish off.
Rnd 4: With **right** side facing, join Ecru with sc in first sc to left of any corner ch-3 sp; ★ † (ch 1, sc in next sc) across to next corner ch-3, working **behind** corner ch-3, (dc, ch 3, dc) in sp before next sc one rnd **below** ch-3 †, sc in next sc; repeat from ★ 2 times **more**, then repeat from † to † once; join with slip st to first sc, finish off.
Rnd 5: With **wrong** side facing, join Green with sc in any corner ch-3 sp; ch 3, sc in same sp, ch 1, skip next dc, (sc in next dc, ch 1) across to within one dc of next corner ch-3 sp, skip next dc, ★ (sc, ch 3, sc) in corner ch-3 sp, ch 1, skip next dc, (sc in next dc, ch 1) across to within one dc of next corner ch-3 sp, skip next dc; repeat from ★ around; join with slip st to first sc, finish off.
Rnds 6-8: Repeat Rnds 4 and 5 once, then repeat Rnd 4 once **more**; at end of Rnd 8, do **not** finish off.
Rnd 9: Slip st in first ch-1 sp, ch 1, ★ † (slip st in next ch-1 sp, ch 1) across to within 2 sts of next corner ch-3 sp, skip next sc, slip st in next dc, ch 1, (slip st, ch 1) twice in corner ch-3 sp, slip st in next dc, ch 1 †, skip next sc; repeat from ★ 2 times **more**, then repeat from † to † once; join with slip st to first slip st, finish off.

To My Brother (continued from page 16)

Row 11: With **right** side facing and large size hook, join Natural with slip st in first st; ch 1, pull up a loop in same st and in next ch-1 sp, YO and draw through all 3 loops on hook, ch 1, (sc in next ch-1 sp, ch 1) 4 times, (sc, ch 3, sc) in next ch-3 sp, ch 1, ★ (sc in next ch-1 sp, ch 1) 5 times, skip next ch-1 sp, (sc in next ch-1 sp, ch 1) 5 times, (sc, ch 3, sc) in next ch-3 sp, ch 1; repeat from ★ across to last 5 ch-1 sps, (sc in next ch-1 sp, ch 1) 4 times, pull up a loop in next ch-1 sp and in last st, YO and draw through all 3 loops on hook; do **not** finish off.
Change to small size hook.
Row 12: Ch 2, turn; dc in first ch-1 sp and in next sc, (dc in next ch-1 sp and in next sc) 4 times, (dc, ch 3, dc) in next ch-3 sp, dc in next sc, (dc in next ch-1 sp and in next sc) 4 times, dc decrease, ★ skip next ch-1 sp, dc decrease, dc in next sc, (dc in next ch-1 sp and in next sc) 4 times, (dc, ch 3, dc) in next ch-3 sp, dc in next sc, (dc in next ch-1 sp and in next sc) 4 times, dc decrease; repeat from ★ across; finish off.
Row 13: With **right** side facing and small size hook, join Burgundy with slip st in first dc; ch 2, dc in next 10 dc, (dc, ch 3, dc) in next ch-3 sp, dc in next 9 dc, ★ dc decrease twice, dc in next 9 dc, (dc, ch 3, dc) in next ch-3 sp, dc in next 9 dc; repeat from ★ across to last 2 dc, dc decrease.
Rows 14-16: Ch 2, turn; dc in next 10 dc, (dc, ch 3, dc) in next ch-3 sp, dc in next 9 dc, ★ dc decrease twice, dc in next 9 dc, (dc, ch 3, dc) in next ch-3 sp, dc in next 9 dc; repeat from ★ across to last 2 dc, dc decrease; at end of Row 16, finish off.
Repeat Rows 5-16, until Afghan measures approximately 71" from beginning ch, ending by working Row 16.

For a Sister (continued from page 18)

Rnd 5: With **right** side facing, join Off-White with slip st in any corner ch-3 sp; ch 3, (2 dc, ch 3, 3 dc) in same sp, ch 1, (3 dc in next ch-1 sp, ch 1) across to next corner ch-3 sp, ★ (3 dc, ch 3, 3 dc) in corner ch-3 sp, ch 1, (3 dc in next ch-1 sp, ch 1) across to next corner ch-3 sp; repeat from ★ 2 times **more**; join with slip st to first dc, finish off: 212 sps.
Rnd 6: With **right** side facing, join Green with slip st in any corner ch-3 sp; ch 4, work (dc, ch 3, V-St) in same sp, ch 1, (work V-St in next ch-1 sp, ch 1) across to next corner ch-3 sp, ★ work (V-St, ch 3, V-St) in corner ch-3 sp, ch 1, (work V-St in next ch-1 sp, ch 1) across to next corner ch-3 sp; repeat from ★ 2 times **more**; join with slip st to third ch of beginning ch-4: 432 sps.

Rnd 7: (Slip st, ch 3, slip st) in first V-St (ch-1 sp), ch 1, slip st in next corner ch-3 sp, (ch 3, slip st in same sp) twice, ch 1, ★ (slip st, ch 3, slip st) in next V-St, ch 1, [(slip st in next ch-1 sp, ch 1, (slip st, ch 3, slip st) in next V-St, ch 1] across to next corner ch-3 sp, slip st in corner ch-3 sp, (ch 3, slip st in same sp) twice, ch 1; repeat from ★ 2 times **more**, [(slip st, ch 3, slip st) in next V-St, ch 1, slip st in next ch-1 sp, ch 1] across; join with slip st to first slip st, finish off.

For an Old-Fashioned Friend (continued from page 20)

PLACEMENT DIAGRAM

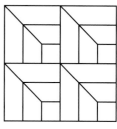

EDGING
Rnd 1: With **right** side facing, join Tan with slip st in top right corner; ch 1, 3 sc in same st, work 23 sc evenly spaced across each Square and 3 sc in each corner st of Afghan; join with slip st to first sc.
Rnd 2: Ch 1, turn; sc in first sc, tr in next sc, (sc in next sc, tr in next sc) around; join with slip st to first sc.
Rnd 3: Ch 1, turn; sc in each st around, working 3 sc in each corner st; join with slip st to first sc.
Rnd 4: Ch 1, turn; sc in first sc, tr in next sc, (sc in next sc, tr in next sc) around; join with slip st to first sc, finish off.

True Blue Friend (continued from page 22)

REMAINING 7 STRIPS
Work same as First Strip through Rnd 5: 186 sps.
Rnd 6 (Joining rnd): Slip st in first ch-2 sp, ch 1, sc in same sp, work Picot, ch 1, sc in next ch-2 sp, work Picot, ch 1, † (dc, ch 1) twice in next dc, tr in next dc, work Picot, ch 1, (dc, ch 1) twice in next dc, (sc in next ch-2 sp, work Picot, ch 1) twice, (sc, ch 3, sc) in next ch-3 sp, 3 dc in next ch-1 sp †, (dc, ch 3, dc) in next ch-3 sp, [dc in next ch-1 sp, (dc, ch 3, dc) in next ch-3 sp] 42 times, 3 dc in next ch-1 sp, (sc, ch 3, sc) in next ch-3 sp, ch 1, (sc in next ch-2 sp, work Picot, ch 1) twice, repeat from † to † once, dc in next ch-3 sp, ch 1, holding Strips with **wrong** sides together, sc in corresponding ch-3 sp on **previous Strip** *(Fig. 24, page 126)*, ch 1, dc in same ch-3 sp on **new Strip**, ★ dc in next ch-1 sp and in next ch-3 sp, ch 1, sc in next ch-3 sp on **previous Strip**, ch 1, dc in same ch-3 sp on **new Strip**; repeat from ★ 41 times **more**, 3 dc in next ch-1 sp, (sc, ch 3, sc) in next ch-3 sp, ch 1; join with slip st to first sc, finish off.

CHART

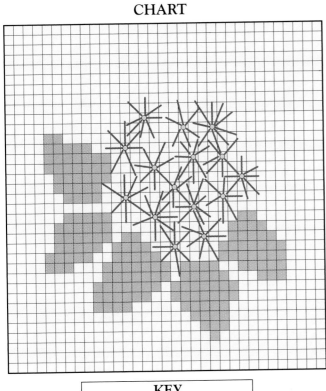

KEY

▨ - Green Cross Stitch

⊙ - Yellow French Knot

◪ - Violet Straight Stitch

With Green, add Cross St leaves **(Fig. 29, page 127)**.
With Yellow, add a French Knot for center of each flower
(Fig. 32, page 127).
With 3 strands of Violet, add Straight St flower petals
(Fig. 30, page 127).

EDGING

With **right** side facing, join Grey with slip st in second ch
of any corner ch-2.

FIRST SIDE
FIRST POINT

Row 1: Ch 1, sc in same st, (sc in next 3 dc and in next ch)
twice: 9 sc.

Rows 2 and 3: Ch 1, turn; work beginning decrease, sc in
each sc across to last 2 sc, work ending decrease: 5 sc.

Row 4: Ch 1, turn; work beginning decrease, sc in next sc,
work ending decrease: 3 sc.

Row 5: Ch 1, turn; pull up a loop in each sc, YO and draw
through all 4 loops on hook: one st.

Row 6: Ch 1, do **not** turn; slip st evenly across end of rows
and in joining; do **not** finish off.

SECOND POINT

Row 1: Slip st in first unworked ch of next Square, ch 1,
do **not** turn; sc in same st, (sc in next 3 dc and in next ch)
twice: 9 sc.

Rows 2-6: Work same as First Point; do **not** finish off.

NEXT POINTS

Repeat Second Point across to last Square on same side
of Afghan.

LAST POINT

Rows 1-5: Work same as Second Point: one st.

Row 6: Ch 1, do **not** turn; slip st evenly across end of
rows, slip st in next unworked ch of corner Square;
do **not** finish off.

REMAINING 3 SIDES

Work same as First Side, ending Last Point of last Side by
working slip st in joining of same corner as first sc;
finish off.

OUTSIDE

Rnd 1: With **right** side facing and large size hook, join
Green with sc in marked ch-5 sp on Circle; ch 3,
(dc, ch 2, dc) in same dc as next 5-dc group, ch 3, ★ sc in
next ch-5 sp, ch 3, (dc, ch 2, dc) in same dc as next
5-dc group, ch 3; repeat from ★ 6 times **more**; join with
slip st to first sc: 24 sts and 24 sps.

Rnd 2: Ch 5, ★ † skip next ch-3 sp, dc in next ch-2 sp,
(ch 1, dc in same sp) 3 times, ch 2, dc in next sc, ch 2,
(sc in next sp, ch 2) 3 times †, dc in next sc, ch 2; repeat
from ★ 2 times **more**, then repeat from † to † once; join
with slip st to third ch of beginning ch-5: 36 sts and 36 sps.

Rnd 3: Ch 1, (sc, hdc) in first ch-2 sp, ★ † dc in next dc and
in next ch-1 sp, (2 dc, ch 1, 2 dc) in next ch-1 sp (corner
made), dc in next ch-1 sp and in next dc, (hdc, sc) in next
ch-2 sp, (3 sc in next ch-2 sp, 2 sc in next ch-2 sp) twice †,
(sc, hdc) in next ch-2 sp; repeat from ★ 2 times **more**, then
repeat from † to † once; join with slip st to first sc, finish off.
Sew Pansy to center of each Square.

SQUARE B (Make 53)

With Green, work same as Background on Square A, page 36.

Instructions continued on page 106.

ASSEMBLY

With Green, using Placement Diagram as a guide, and working through inside loops only, whipstitch Squares together forming strips (**Fig. 26a, page 126**), beginning in first corner ch and ending in next corner ch; whipstitch strips together in same manner.

PLACEMENT DIAGRAM

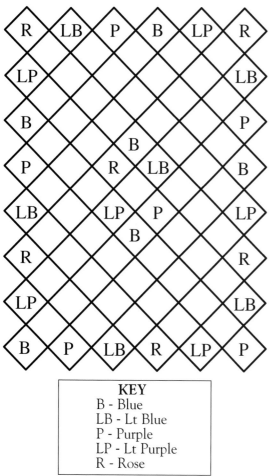

KEY
B - Blue
LB - Lt Blue
P - Purple
LP - Lt Purple
R - Rose

EDGING

With large size hook, join Dk Green with slip st in any outside corner ch-1 sp; ch 2, 2 hdc in same sp, hdc evenly around, working 3 hdc in ch-1 sp at each point and decrease in each valley; join with slip st to top of beginning ch-2, finish off.

REVERSIBLE PLAID

Finished Size: 48" x 67"

MATERIALS

Worsted Weight Yarn:
Red - 29 ounces, (820 grams, 1,905 yards)
Blue - 6 ounces, (170 grams, 395 yards)
White - 4½ ounces, (130 grams, 295 yards)
Yellow - 3 ounces, (90 grams, 200 yards)
Green - 2½ ounces, (70 grams, 165 yards)
Crochet hook, size H (5.00 mm) **or** size needed for gauge

GAUGE: 15 tr and 5 rows = 4"

Gauge Swatch: 4" square
Ch 18 **loosely**.
Row 1: Tr in fifth ch from hook (**4 skipped chs count as first tr**) and in each ch across: 15 tr.
Rows 2-5: Ch 4 (**counts as first tr**), turn; tr in next tr and in each tr across.
Finish off.

AFGHAN BODY

With Red, ch 184 **loosely**.
Row 1 (Right side): Tr in fifth ch from hook (**4 skipped chs count as first tr**), tr in next 8 chs, ★ † ch 2, skip next 2 chs, tr in next 7 chs, ch 2, (skip next 2 chs, tr in next ch, ch 2) twice, skip next 2 chs †, tr in next 31 chs, ch 2, skip next 2 chs, tr in next ch, ch 2, skip next 2 chs, tr in next 19 chs; repeat from ★ once **more**, then repeat from † to † once, tr in each ch across: 149 tr.
Note: Loop a short piece of yarn around any stitch to mark Row 1 as **right** side and bottom edge.
Row 2: Ch 4 (**counts as first tr, now and throughout**), turn; tr in next 9 tr, ★ † ch 2, (skip next ch-2 sp, tr in next tr, ch 2) twice, skip next ch-2 sp, tr in next 7 tr, ch 2, skip next ch-2 sp †, tr in next 19 tr, ch 2, skip next ch-2 sp, tr in next tr, ch 2, skip next ch-2 sp, tr in next 31 tr; repeat from ★ once **more**, then repeat from † to † once, tr in each st across.
Row 3: Ch 4, turn; tr in next 9 tr, ★ † ch 2, skip next ch-2 sp, tr in next 7 tr, ch 2, (skip next ch-2 sp, tr in next tr, ch 2) twice, skip next ch-2 sp †, tr in next 31 tr, ch 2, skip next ch-2 sp, tr in next tr, ch 2, skip next ch-2 sp, tr in next 19 tr; repeat from ★ once **more**, then repeat from † to † once, tr in each tr across.
Row 4: Repeat Row 2.

Row 5 (Eyelet row): Ch 6 **(counts as first tr plus ch 2, now and throughout)**, turn; skip next 2 tr, tr in next tr, (ch 2, skip next 2 tr, tr in next tr) twice, ★ † ch 2, skip next ch-2 sp, tr in next tr, (ch 2, skip next 2 tr, tr in next tr) twice, (ch 2, skip next ch-2 sp, tr in next tr) 3 times †, (ch 2, skip next 2 tr, tr in next tr) 10 times, (ch 2, skip next ch-2 sp, tr in next tr) twice, (ch 2, skip next 2 tr, tr in next tr) 6 times; repeat from ★ once **more**, then repeat from † to † once, (ch 2, skip next 2 tr, tr in next tr) across: 60 ch-2 sps.

Rows 6 and 7 (Eyelet rows): Ch 6, turn; skip next ch-2 sp, tr in next tr, (ch 2, skip next ch-2 sp, tr in next tr) across.

Row 8: Ch 4, turn; (tr in next 2 chs, tr in next tr) 3 times, ★ † (ch 2, skip next ch-2 sp, tr in next tr) 3 times, (tr in next 2 chs, tr in next tr) twice, ch 2, skip next ch-2 sp, tr in next tr †, (tr in next 2 chs, tr in next tr) 6 times, (ch 2, skip next ch-2 sp, tr in next tr) twice, (tr in next 2 chs, tr in next tr) 10 times; repeat from ★ once **more**, then repeat from † to † once, (tr in next 2 chs, tr in next tr) across: 149 tr.

Rows 9-17: Repeat Row 3 once, then repeat Rows 2 and 3, 4 times.

Row 18 (Eyelet row): Ch 6, turn; skip next 2 tr, tr in next tr, (ch 2, skip next 2 tr, tr in next tr) twice, ★ † (ch 2, skip next ch-2 sp, tr in next tr) 3 times, (ch 2, skip next 2 tr, tr in next tr) twice, ch 2, skip next ch-2 sp, tr in next tr †, (ch 2, skip next 2 tr, tr in next tr) 6 times, (ch 2, skip next ch-2 sp, tr in next tr) twice, (ch 2, skip next 2 tr, tr in next tr) 10 times; repeat from ★ once **more**, then repeat from † to † once, (ch 2, skip next 2 tr, tr in next tr) across: 60 ch-2 sps.

Rows 19 and 20: Repeat Rows 7 and 8.

Rows 21-25: Repeat Row 3 once, then repeat Rows 2 and 3 twice.

Row 26: Repeat Row 18.

Row 27: Ch 4, turn; (tr in next 2 chs, tr in next tr) 3 times, ★ † ch 2, skip next ch-2 sp, tr in next tr, (tr in next 2 chs, tr in next tr) twice, (ch 2, skip next ch-2 sp, tr in next tr) 3 times †, (tr in next 2 chs, tr in next tr) 10 times, (ch 2, skip next ch-2 sp, tr in next tr) twice, (tr in next 2 chs, tr in next tr) 6 times; repeat from ★ once **more**, then repeat from † to † once, (tr in next 2 chs, tr in next tr) across.

Row 28: Repeat Row 2.

Rows 29-83: Repeat Rows 5-28 twice, then repeat Rows 5-11 once **more**.
Finish off.

STRIPES

Note: Always join yarn and finish off leaving a 4" end for fringe.

Referring to Placement Diagram for color placement, work all Vertical Lines of one color and then all Horizontal Lines of the same color. Work colors in the following sequence: White, Blue, Yellow, Green.

VERTICAL LINE

Front Stripe: Hold afghan with **right** side facing and top edge toward you; working upward, join yarn with slip st around first ch-2; (ch 3 **loosely**, sc around next skipped ch-2) across; finish off.

Back Stripe: Hold afghan with **wrong** side facing and bottom edge toward you; working to **left** of Front Stripe and around same skipped ch-2, join yarn with slip st around skipped ch-2 of beginning ch; working upward, (ch 3 **loosely**, sc around next skipped ch-2) across; finish off.

HORIZONTAL LINE

Front Stripe: Hold afghan with **right** side facing and bottom edge toward the left; join yarn with slip st around post of first tr of Eyelet row; working upward, (ch 3 **loosely**, sc around post of next tr) across; finish off.

Back Stripe: Hold afghan with **wrong** side facing and bottom edge toward the left; working to **right** of Front Stripe and around same tr, join yarn with slip st around post of first tr; working upward, (ch 3 **loosely**, sc around post of next tr) across; finish off.

Using 3 strands of matching color, add additional 4" fringe to end of every Stripe Line around Afghan **(Figs. 27a & b, page 126)**, using 4 strands of Red, add 4" fringe to short edges of Afghan, evenly spacing fringe between Stripes.

PLACEMENT DIAGRAM

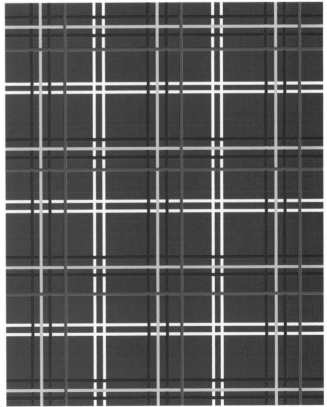

CHART

-Row 125
-Row 121
-Row 111
-Row 101
-Row 91
-Row 81
-Row 71
-Row 61
-Row 51
-Row 41
-Row 31
-Row 21
-Row 11
-Row 3
-Row 1 (Right side)

KEY

■ - Block

□ - Space

CHART

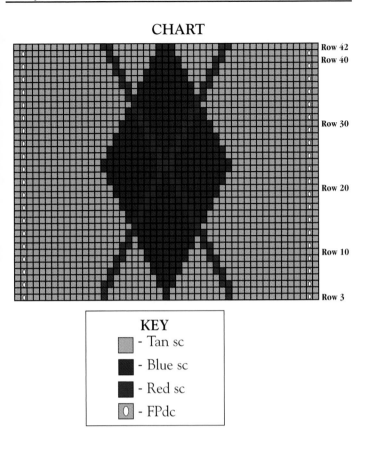

Row 42
Row 40

Row 30

Row 20

Row 10

Row 3

KEY

- Tan sc
- Blue sc
- Red sc
- FPdc

You Are My Sunshine (continued from page 44)

ASSEMBLY

With Dk Green, using Placement Diagram as a guide, and working through both loops, whipstitch Squares together *(Fig. 26b, page 126)*, forming 7 vertical strips of 9 Squares each, beginning in center ch of first corner ch-3 and ending in center ch of next corner ch-3; whipstitch strips together in same manner.

PLACEMENT DIAGRAM

A	B	A	B	A	B	A
B	A	B	A	B	A	B
A	B	A	B	A	B	A
B	A	B	A	B	A	B
A	B	A	B	A	B	A
B	A	B	A	B	A	B
A	B	A	B	A	B	A
B	A	B	A	B	A	B
A	B	A	B	A	B	A

EDGING

Rnd 1: With **right** side facing, join Dk Green with slip st in any corner ch-3 sp; ch 1, (sc, ch 3, sc) in same sp, ★ † sc in next 25 dc, (sc in next 2 sps and in next 25 dc) across to next corner ch-3 sp †, (sc, ch 3, sc) in corner ch-3 sp; repeat from ★ 2 times **more**, then repeat from † to † once; join with slip st to first sc: 864 sc.

Rnd 2: Slip st in first ch-3 sp, ch 1, (sc, ch 3, sc) in same sp, ch 3, skip next sc, (sc in next sc, ch 3, skip next sc) across to next corner ch-3 sp, ★ (sc, ch 3, sc) in corner ch-3 sp, ch 3, skip next sc, (sc in next sc, ch 3, skip next sc) across to next corner ch-3 sp; repeat from ★ around; join with slip st to first sc, finish off.

Wedding (continued from page 52)

Rnd 8: Ch 1, turn; working in both loops, sc in next 4 sc, working in **front** of next sc, dc in free loop of ch one rnd **below** sc *(Fig. 21a, page 125)*, skip next sc, sc in next 2 sc, (2 sc, ch 3, 2 sc) in next ch-3 sp, sc in next 2 sc, working in **front** of next sc, dc in free loop of ch one rnd **below** sc, sc in next 6 sc, ★ † working in **front** of next sc, dc in free loop of sc one rnd **below** sc, skip next sc, sc in next 6 sc †, repeat from † to † once **more**, working in **front** of next sc, dc in free loop of ch one rnd **below** sc, skip next sc, sc in next 2 sc, (2 sc, ch 3, 2 sc) in next ch-3 sp, sc in next 2 sc, working in **front** of next sc, dc in free loop of ch one rnd **below** sc, sc in next 6 sc; repeat from ★ 2 times **more**, then repeat from † to † once, working in **front** of next sc, dc in free loop of sc one rnd **below** sc, skip next sc, sc in last 2 sc; join with slip st to Back Loop Only of first sc: 120 sts and 4 ch-3 sps.

Rnd 9: Ch 1, turn; working in Front Loops Only, sc in next 21 sts and in next ch, (sc, ch 3, sc) in next ch, sc in next ch, ★ sc in next 30 sts and in next ch, (sc, ch 3, sc) in next ch, sc in next ch; repeat from ★ 2 times **more**, sc in last 9 sts; join with slip st to **both** loops of first sc: 136 sc and 4 ch-3 sps.

Rnd 10: Ch 1, turn; working in both loops, sc in next 4 sc, working in **front** of next sc, dc in free loop of dc one rnd **below** sc, skip next sc, sc in next 6 sc and in next 2 chs; ch 6 **loosely**, working in back ridge of chs *(Fig. 2b, page 122)*, slip st in second ch from hook and in next 2 chs, sc in next ch, hdc in last ch, sc in same corner ch and in next ch, ★ † sc in next 6 sc, working in **front** of next sc, dc in free loop of dc one rnd **below** sc, skip next sc †, repeat from † to † 3 times **more**, sc in next 6 sc and in next 2 chs; ch 6 **loosely**, working in back ridge of chs, slip st in second ch from hook and in next 2 chs, sc in next ch, hdc in last ch, sc in same corner ch and in next ch; repeat from ★ 2 times **more**, then repeat from † to † 3 times, sc in last 2 sc; join with slip st to first sc, finish off.

Instructions continued on page 110.

OVAL (Make 31)
CENTER

Note: Rnds 1-5 of Center are worked in continuous rnds. Place a 2" scrap piece of yarn in last sc made to mark end of rnd, moving marker to last st of next rnd as rnd is completed.

With Ecru, ch 18 **loosely**.

Rnd 1: (Sc, ch 1, sc) in second ch from hook, sc in next 15 chs, (sc, ch 1, sc) in last ch; working in free loops of beginning ch **(Fig. 21b, page 125)**, sc in next 15 chs; do **not** join, place marker: 34 sc and 2 ch-1 sps.

Note: Work in Back Loops Only throughout.

Rnd 2: Sc in next sc, 3 sc in next ch, sc in next 17 sc, 3 sc in next ch, sc in next 16 sc: 40 sc.

Rnd 3: Sc in next 2 sc, 3 sc in next sc, sc in next 5 sc, hdc in next 3 sc, dc in next 3 sc, hdc in next 3 sc, sc in next 5 sc, 3 sc in next sc, sc in next 5 sc, hdc in next 3 sc, dc in next 3 sc, hdc in next 3 sc, sc in next 3 sc: 44 sts.

Rnd 4: Sc in next 3 sc, (sc, ch 3, sc) in next sc, sc in next 21 sts, (sc, ch 3, sc) in next sc, sc in next 18 sts: 46 sts and 2 ch-3 sps.

Rnd 5 (Right side): Sc in next 4 sc and in next ch, (sc, ch 1, sc) in next ch, sc in next ch, sc in next 23 sc and in next ch, (sc, ch 1, sc) in next ch, sc in next ch and in next 19 sc, remove marker; slip st in next sc, finish off: 54 sc and 2 ch-1 sps.

Note: Loop a short piece of yarn around any stitch to mark Rnd 5 as **right** side.

FIRST SIDE

Row 1: With **wrong** side of Center facing, join Pink with sc in first ch-1 sp (corner) **(see Joining With Sc, page 125)**; sc in Front Loop Only of next 27 sc, sc in next ch-1 sp, leave remaining sts unworked: 29 sc.

Row 2: Ch 1, turn; working in both loops, sc in first 4 sc, working in **front** of next sc, dc in free loop of sc one rnd **below** sc, ★ sc in next 4 sc, working in **front** of next sc, dc in free loop of sc one rnd **below** sc; repeat from ★ 4 times **more**, skip next sc, sc in last 4 sc changing to Purple in last sc **(Fig. 22a, page 125)**: 34 sts.

Row 3: Ch 1, turn; sc in Front Loop Only of each st across.

Row 4: Ch 1, turn; working in both loops, sc in first 4 sc, ★ working in **front** of next sc, dc in free loop of dc one row **below** sc, skip sc behind dc, sc in next 4 sc; repeat from ★ across changing to Green in last sc.

Row 5: Ch 1, turn; sc in Front Loop Only of each st across.

Row 6: Ch 1, turn; working in both loops, sc in first 3 sc, 2 sc in next sc, ★ working in **front** of next sc, dc in free loop of dc one row **below** sc, sc in next 5 sc; repeat from ★ across changing to Pink in last sc: 41 sts.

Row 7: Ch 1, turn; sc in Front Loop Only of each st across.

Row 8: Ch 1, turn; working in both loops, sc in first 5 sc, ★ working in **front** of next sc, dc in free loop of dc one row **below** sc, skip sc behind dc, sc in next 5 sc; repeat from ★ across changing to Purple in last sc.

Row 9: Ch 1, turn; sc in Front Loop Only of each st across.

Row 10: Ch 1, turn; working in both loops, sc in first 4 sc, 2 sc in next sc, ★ working in **front** of next sc, dc in free loop of dc one row **below** sc, sc in next 6 sc; repeat from ★ across; finish off: 48 sts.

SECOND SIDE

Row 1: With **wrong** side of Center facing, join Pink with sc in same ch-1 sp as last sc made on First Side; sc in Front Loop Only of next 27 sc, sc in next ch-1 sp: 29 sc.

Rows 2-10: Work same as First Side.

ASSEMBLY

Using Placement Diagram as a guide and working through inside loops only, whipstitch pieces together as follows **(Fig. 26a, page 126)**:

With Purple, whipstitch a Purple Square to each end of 16 Ovals.

With Pink, whipstitch a Pink Square to **each** end of 15 Ovals.

With Ecru, whipstitch Ovals to Diamonds.

With Purple, whipstitch Squares to Squares.

PLACEMENT DIAGRAM

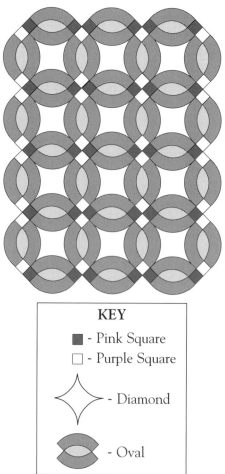

KEY
■ - Pink Square
□ - Purple Square
◇ - Diamond
⬯ - Oval

EDGING

Rnd 1: With **wrong** side facing and working in Front Loops Only, join Ecru with sc in any st; dc in next st, (sc in next st, dc in next st) around; join with slip st to **both** loops of first sc.

Rnd 2: Ch 3, working in both loops, sc in next dc, (dc in next sc, sc in next dc) around; join with slip st to top of beginning ch-3.

Rnd 3: Turn; slip st **loosely** in Front Loop Only of each st around; join with slip st to first slip st, finish off.

Heartfelt Thank-You (continued from page 54)

EDGING
FIRST SIDE

With **right** side facing, join Ecru with slip st in first sc on Row 183; ch 2, dc in same st, (slip st, ch 2, dc) in each sc across to last sc, slip st in last sc; finish off.

SECOND SIDE

With **right** side facing and working in free loops of beginning ch **(Fig. 21b, page 125)**, join Ecru with slip st in first ch; ch 2, dc in same ch, skip next 2 chs, ★ (slip st, ch 2, dc) in next ch, skip next 2 chs; repeat from ★ 87 times **more**, slip st in next ch; finish off.

Holding 2 strands of corresponding color together, add additional 9" fringe evenly across short edges of Afghan **(Figs. 27a & b, page 126)**.

A Homemade Friend (continued from page 59)

Rnd 8: Ch 3, dc in next dc, work FPdc around next FPdc, (dc in next 2 dc, work FPdc around next FPdc) 3 times, ★ YO, insert hook from **front** to **back** around second leg of **next** st, YO and pull up a loop, YO and draw through 2 loops on hook; repeat from ★ 2 times **more**, YO and draw through all 4 loops on hook, work FPdc around second leg of next st, (dc in next 2 dc, work FPdc around next FPdc) twice; join with slip st to first dc: 20 sts.

Rnd 9: Ch 3, dc in next dc, work FPdc around next FPdc, (dc in next 2 dc, work FPdc around next FPdc) 3 times, 2 dc in next st, work FPdc around next FPdc, (dc in next 2 dc, work FPdc around next FPdc) twice; join with slip st to first dc: 21 sts.

Rnds 10-16: Ch 3, dc in next dc, work FPdc around next FPdc, (dc in next 2 dc, work FPdc around next FPdc) around; join with slip st to first dc.
Stuff Leg lightly with polyester fiberfill.

Rnd 17: Ch 2, dc in next dc, work FPdc around next FPdc, (decrease, work FPdc around next FPdc) around; join with slip st to first dc, finish off leaving a long end for sewing.
Thread yarn needle with long end and weave through remaining sts on Rnd 17; gather tightly and secure end.

EAR (Make 2)

With Brown, ch 7 **loosely**.

Rnd 1 (Right side): 2 Dc in fourth ch from hook **(3 skipped chs count as first dc)**, 3 dc in each of next 3 chs; working in free loops of beginning ch, 3 dc in each of next 2 chs; join with slip st to first dc: 18 dc.

Rnd 2: Ch 3, dc in next dc, work FPdc around next dc, skip dc behind FPdc, ★ dc in next 2 dc, work FPdc around next dc, skip dc behind FPdc; repeat from ★ around; join with slip st to first dc.

Rnd 3: Ch 3, dc in next dc, work FPdc around next FPdc, (dc in next 2 dc, work FPdc around next FPdc) around; join with slip st to first dc, finish off leaving a long end for sewing.

Thread yarn needle with long end; using photo as a guide for placement, flatten and cup Ears and sew to top of Head.

FINISHING

Using photo as a guide for placement:
Sew inside of Rnd 12 of Arms to Rnd 3 of Body. Sew inside of Rnd 15 of Legs to Rnd 11 of Body.
Sew button to Head for eyes; sew 2 buttons to front of Body. With Black, add satin stitch for nose **(Fig. 31, page 127)** and add straight stitch for mouth **(Fig. 30, page 127)**.
Tie ribbon into a bow around neck.

Birthday Wishes (continued from page 60)

> ### FRONT POST DOUBLE CROCHET
> **(abbreviated FPdc)**
> YO, insert hook from **front** to **back** around post of dc indicated, YO and pull up a loop **(Fig. 11, page 123)**, (YO and draw through 2 loops on hook) twice. Skip st behind FPdc.
>
> ### BEGINNING SPLIT TREBLE CROCHET
> **(abbreviated Beginning Split tr)**
> YO twice, insert hook from **back** to **front** in skipped FPdc **(Fig. 1a)**, YO and pull up a loop, (YO and draw through 2 loops on hook) twice, YO twice, skip next 2 dc, insert hook from **front** to **back** in next FPdc **(Fig. 1b)**, YO and pull up a loop, (YO and draw through 2 loops on hook) twice, YO and draw through all 3 loops on hook.
>
> **Fig. 1a** **Fig. 1b**
>
>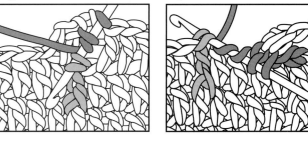
>
> *Stitch Guide continued on page 112.*

Birthday Wishes (continued from page 111)

SPLIT TREBLE CROCHET (abbreviated Split tr)

YO twice, insert hook from **back** to **front** in same FPdc as last Split tr made **(Fig. 2a)**, YO and pull up a loop, (YO and draw through 2 loops on hook) twice, YO twice, skip next 2 dc, insert hook from **front** to **back** in next FPdc **(Fig. 2b)**, YO and pull up a loop, (YO and draw through 2 loops on hook) twice, YO and draw through all 3 loops on hook.

Fig. 2a   **Fig. 2b**

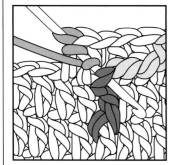 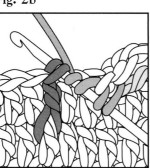

ENDING SPLIT TREBLE CROCHET
  (abbreviated Ending Split tr)

YO twice, insert hook from **back** to **front** in same FPdc as last Split tr made, YO and pull up a loop, (YO and draw through 2 loops on hook) twice, YO twice, working in **front** of first 2 dc, insert hook from **front** to **back** in same FPdc as Beginning Split tr, YO and pull up a loop, (YO and draw through 2 loops on hook) twice, YO and draw through all 3 loops on hook.

A Good Friend (continued from page 62)

PLACEMENT DIAGRAM

Baby Shower (continued from page 64)

BORDER

Rnd 1: With **right** side facing, join Pink with sc in corner ch-5 sp of either Pink corner Motif **(see Joining With Sc, page 125)**; ★ † ch 3, (sc in next ch-3 sp, ch 3) 3 times, [sc in next joining sc, ch 3, (sc in next ch-3 sp, ch 3) 3 times] 3 times †, sc in next corner ch-5 sp; repeat from ★ 2 times **more**, then repeat from † to † once; join with slip st to first sc: 64 ch-3 sps.

Rnd 2: Slip st in first ch-3 sp, ch 1, sc in same sp, ch 3, (sc in next ch-3 sp, ch 3) around; join with slip st to first sc, finish off.

Rnd 3: With **right** side facing, join White with sc in ch-3 sp to right of joining; ch 3, (sc in next ch-3 sp, ch 3) 15 times, ★ (sc, ch 5, sc) in next ch-3 sp, ch 3, (sc in next ch-3 sp, ch 3) 15 times; repeat from ★ 2 times **more**, sc in same sp as first sc, ch 5; join with slip st to first sc: 64 ch-3 sps and 4 ch-5 sps.

Rnd 4: Slip st in first ch-3 sp, ch 1, sc in same sp, ch 5, ★ (sc in next ch-3 sp, ch 5) across to next corner ch-5 sp, (sc, ch 7, sc) in corner ch-5 sp, ch 5; repeat from ★ around; join with slip st to first sc, finish off: 72 sps.

Place one Pillow Square on top of the other with **right** side of **each** facing **up**; pin to hold layers together.

REMAINING 11 SQUARES

Work same as Pillow Square, page 64, through Rnd 3 of Border beginning Rnd 1 of Border for Squares 3-11 in corner ch-5 sp of either Green corner Motif: 64 ch-3 sps and 4 ch-5 sps.

Note: Refer to Assembly and Placement Diagram, page 113, and join Motifs in numerical order.

Rnd 4 (Joining rnd): Work One or Two Side Joining.

ONE SIDE JOINING

Rnd 4 (Joining rnd): Slip st in first ch-3 sp, ch 1, sc in same sp, ch 5, (sc in next ch-3 sp, ch 5) across to next corner ch-5 sp, ★ (sc, ch 7, sc) in corner ch-5 sp, ch 5, (sc in next ch-3 sp, ch 5) across to next corner ch-5 sp; repeat from ★ once **more**, sc in corner ch-5 sp, ch 3, holding Squares with **wrong** sides together, sc in corresponding corner ch-7 sp on **adjacent** Square, ch 3, sc in same sp on **new** Square, ch 2, sc in next ch-5 sp on **adjacent** Square, ch 2, (sc in next ch-3 sp on **new** Square, ch 2, sc in next ch-5 sp on **adjacent** Square, ch 2) across to next corner ch-5 sp on **new** Square, sc in corner ch-5 sp, ch 3, sc in corner ch-7 sp on **adjacent** Square, ch 3, sc in same sp on **new** Square, ch 5; join with slip st to first sc, finish off.

TWO SIDE JOINING

Rnd 4 (Joining rnd): Slip st in first ch-3 sp, ch 1, sc in same sp, ch 5, (sc in next ch-3 sp, ch 5) across to next corner ch-5 sp, (sc, ch 7, sc) in corner ch-5 sp, ch 5, (sc in next ch-3 sp, ch 5) across to next corner ch-5 sp, sc in corner ch-5 sp, ch 3, holding Squares with **wrong** sides together, sc in corresponding corner ch-7 sp on **adjacent Square**, ch 3, sc in same sp on **new Square**, † ch 2, sc in next ch-5 sp on **adjacent Square**, ch 2, (sc in next ch-3 sp on **new Square**, ch 2, sc in next ch-5 sp on **adjacent Square**, ch 2) across to next corner ch-5 sp on **new Square**, sc in corner ch-5 sp, ch 3 †, sc in each of next 3 corner sps on **adjacent Squares**, ch 3, sc in same sp on **new Square**, repeat from † to † once, sc in corner ch-7 sp on **adjacent Square**, ch 3, sc in same sp on **new Square**, ch 5; join with slip st to first sc, finish off.

ASSEMBLY

Referring to Placement Diagram, join Squares 1 and 2 to the Pillow Squares, working through **both** Pillow Squares. When joining Square 4 to the Pillow Square, **work through top Pillow Square only**, leaving the **top** edge of bottom Pillow Square unjoined to be used for pocket.

PLACEMENT DIAGRAM

9	10	11
6	7	8
3	4	5
1	Pillow Squares	2

EDGING

With **right** side facing and working through **both** Pillow Squares along bottom edge, join White with sc in any corner ch-7 sp; ch 7, sc in same sp, ch 5, (sc in next ch-5 sp, ch 5) across to next corner ch-7 sp, ★ (sc, ch 7, sc) in corner ch-7 sp, ch 5, (sc in next ch-5 sp, ch 5) across to next corner ch-7 sp; repeat from ★ 2 times **more**; join with slip st to first sc, finish off.

FOLDING INSTRUCTIONS

Lay Afghan **right** side up on a flat surface. The grey square in Fig. 1 indicates the pillow squares that form the pocket. Fold the two outside vertical strips over the center strip and then fold from top to bottom, ending over the pocket. Turn the pocket **over** the folded Afghan to form pillow **(Fig. 1)**.

Fig. 1

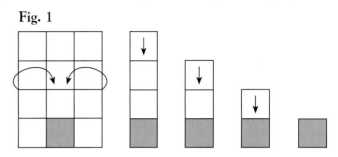

Thoughts of You (continued from page 66)

Rnd 3: Ch 6, tr in next tr, (ch 2, tr in next tr) 7 times, † ch 2, dc in next dc, ch 2, [tr in next tr, (ch 1, tr in next tr) 6 times, ch 2, dc in next dc, ch 2] 16 times, tr in next tr, (ch 2, tr in next tr) 8 times, ch 2, dc in next dc, ch 2, [tr in next tr, (ch 1, tr in next tr) 6 times, ch 2, dc in next dc, ch 2] 22 times †, tr in next tr, (ch 2, tr in next tr) 8 times, repeat from † to † once; join with slip st to fourth ch of beginning ch-6.

Rnd 4: Ch 7, slip st in third ch from hook, (ch 2, tr in next tr, work Picot) 8 times, † ch 4, sc in next dc, ch 4, [tr in next tr, work Picot, (ch 1, tr in next tr, work Picot) 6 times, ch 4, sc in next dc, ch 4] 16 times, tr in next tr, work Picot, (ch 2, tr in next tr, work Picot) 8 times, ch 4, sc in next dc, ch 4, [tr in next tr, work Picot, (ch 1, tr in next tr, work Picot) 6 times, ch 4, sc in next dc, ch 4] 22 times †, tr in next tr, work Picot, (ch 2, tr in next tr, work Picot) 8 times, repeat from † to † once; join with slip st to fourth ch of beginning ch-7, finish off.

Housewarming (continued from page 70)

Rnd 10: Ch 3, dc in next 2 dc and in next ch-1 sp, (dc in next dc, ch 1) twice, dc in next dc and in next ch-1 sp, dc in next 5 dc, (ch 1, dc in next dc) twice, (2 dc, ch 3, 2 dc) in next corner ch-3 sp, ★ † (dc in next dc, ch 1) twice, dc in next 5 dc and in next ch-1 sp, (dc in next dc, ch 1) twice, dc in next dc and in next ch-1 sp †, dc in next 3 dc and in next ch-1 sp, dc in next dc, (ch 1, dc in next dc) twice, dc in next ch-1 sp and in next 5 dc, (ch 1, dc in next dc) twice, (2 dc, ch 3, 2 dc) in next corner ch-3 sp; repeat from ★ 2 times **more**, then repeat from † to † once; join with slip st to first dc, do **not** finish off: 124 dc and 36 sps.

Instructions continued on page 114.

Housewarming (continued from page 113)

Rnd 11: Ch 3, dc in next 4 dc and in next ch-1 sp, dc in next dc and in next ch-1 sp, dc in next 7 dc, ★ † ch 1, dc in next dc, ch 1, dc in next 3 dc, (2 dc, ch 3, 2 dc) in next corner ch-3 sp, dc in next 3 dc, ch 1, dc in next dc, ch 1, dc in next 7 dc †, (dc in next ch-1 sp and in next dc, dc in next ch-1 sp and in next 7 dc) twice; repeat from ★ 2 times **more**, then repeat from † to † once, dc in next ch-1 sp and in next dc, dc in next ch-1 sp and in last 2 dc; join with slip st to first dc, finish off: 156 dc and 20 sps.

ASSEMBLY

Working through both loops, whipstitch Squares together (*Fig. 26b, page 126*), forming 4 vertical strips of 5 Squares each, beginning in center ch of first corner ch-3 and ending in center ch of next corner ch-3; whipstitch strips together in same manner.

EDGING

Rnd 1: With **right** side facing, join yarn with slip st in any corner ch-3 sp; ch 6 **(counts as first dc plus ch 3)**, dc in same sp, ★ † ch 1, dc in next dc, ch 1, (skip next st, dc in next dc, ch 1) 21 times, [(dc in next sp, ch 1) twice, dc in next dc, ch 1, (skip next st, dc in next dc, ch 1) 21 times] across to next corner ch-3 sp †, (dc, ch 3, dc) in corner ch-3 sp; repeat from ★ 2 times **more**, then repeat from † to † once; join with slip st to first dc: 432 dc.
Rnd 2: Ch 4, (dc, ch 3, dc) in first corner ch-3 sp, ch 1, ★ (dc in next dc, ch 1) across to next corner ch-3 sp, (dc, ch 3, dc) in corner ch-3 sp, ch 1; repeat from ★ 2 times **more**, (dc in next dc, ch 1) across; join with slip st to first dc: 440 dc.
Rnd 3: Ch 2, slip st in next dc, ch 2, (slip st, ch 3, slip st) in next corner ch-3 sp, ch 2, ★ (slip st in next dc, ch 2) across to next corner ch-3 sp, (slip st, ch 3, slip st) in corner ch-3 sp, ch 2; repeat from ★ 2 times **more**, (slip st in next dc, ch 2) across; join with slip st to first slip st, finish off.

Get Well Soon (continued from page 72)

Rnd 9: With **right** side facing, join Ecru with slip st in first sc; ch 5, dtr in same st and in next sc, ★ † tr in next 2 sc, dc in next 4 sc, skip next sc, dc in next sc, hdc in next sc, sc in next 5 sc, hdc in next sc, dc in next sc, skip next sc, dc in next 4 sc, tr in next 2 sc, dtr in next sc †, 2 dtr in next sc, dtr in next sc; repeat from ★ 2 times **more**, then repeat from † to † once; join with slip st to top of beginning ch-5: 100 sts.
Rnd 10: Working in both loops, ch 3, (tr, dtr) in same st, (dtr, tr, dc) in next st, dc in next 23 sts, ★ (dc, tr, dtr) in next st, (dtr, tr, dc) in next st, dc in next 23 sts; repeat from ★ around; join with slip st to top of beginning ch-3, finish off: 116 sts.

SQUARE B (Make 17)

Work same as Square A, working Rnd 6 with Ecru and Rnds 9 and 10 with Tan.

ASSEMBLY

With Ecru and working through inside loops only, whipstitch Squares together (*Fig. 26a, page 126*), forming 5 vertical strips of 7 Squares each, alternating Square A with Square B and beginning in first dtr and ending in last dtr on each side; whipstitch strips together in same manner, securing seam at each joining.

EDGING

Note: Work in Back Loops Only throughout.
Rnd 1: With **right** side facing, skip 2 dtr on any corner and join Lt Blue with slip st in next tr; ch 1, 2 sc in same st, ★ † (sc in each st across to next joining, dc in joining) across to last Square, sc in next 28 sts, (sc, hdc, dc) in next dtr, (dc, hdc, sc) in next dtr †, 2 sc in next tr; repeat from ★ 2 times **more**, then repeat from † to † once; join with slip st to first sc changing to Ecru (*Fig. 22b, page 125*): 736 sts.
Rnd 2: Ch 3, hdc in same st, ★ † (hdc, sc) in next sc, sc in next sc, decrease, sc in next st, (hdc in next st, dc in next st, 2 tr in each of next 2 sts, dc in next st, hdc in next st, sc in next st, decrease, sc in next sc) across to within 3 sts of next hdc at corner, (sc, hdc) in next sc, (hdc, dc) in next sc, dc in next sc, (dc, tr) in next hdc, tr in next 2 dc, (tr, dc) in next hdc, dc in next sc †, (dc, hdc) in next sc; repeat from ★ 2 times **more**, then repeat from † to † once; join with slip st to top of beginning ch-3 changing to Blue: 824 sts.
Rnd 3: Ch 1, sc in same st and in next 4 sts, ★ † (skip next sc, sc in next 4 sts, 2 sc in each of next 2 tr, sc in next 4 sts) across to within 8 sts of next tr at corner, skip next sc, sc in next 8 sts, 2 sc in each of next 2 tr †, sc in next 8 sts; repeat from ★ 2 times **more**, then repeat from † to † once, sc in last 3 sts; join with slip st to first sc changing to Maroon: 896 sc.
Rnd 4: Ch 1, sc in same st and in next 3 sc, ★ † (skip next 2 sc, sc in next 4 sc, 2 sc in each of next 2 sc, sc in next 4 sc) across to within 9 sts of next 2-sc group at corner, skip next 2 sc, sc in next 8 sc, 2 sc in each of next 2 sc †, sc in next 8 sc; repeat from ★ 2 times **more**, then repeat from † to † once, sc in last 4 sc; join with slip st to first sc changing to Tan.
Rnd 5: Ch 2, ★ † dc in next 2 sc, tr in next 2 sc, dc in next 2 sc, hdc in next sc, (sc in next sc, decrease, sc in next sc, hdc in next sc, dc in next 2 sc, tr in next 2 sc, dc in next 2 sc, hdc in next sc) across to within 4 sts of next 2-sc group at corner, sc in next 2 sc, hdc in next sc, dc in next sc, (dc, tr) in next sc, tr in next 2 sc, (tr, dc) in next sc, dc in next sc, hdc in next sc, sc in next 2 sc †, hdc in next sc; repeat from ★ 2 times **more**, then repeat from † to † once; join with slip st to top of beginning ch-2, finish off.

MOROCCAN TILE PILLOW

Finished Size: 12" square

MATERIALS
Worsted Weight Yarn:
    Ecru - 1½ ounces, (40 grams, 105 yards)
    Tan - 1 ounce, (30 grams, 70 yards)
    Maroon - 1 ounce, (30 grams, 70 yards)
    Lt Blue - ½ ounce, (15 grams, 35 yards)
    Blue - 1 ounce, (30 grams, 70 yards)
    Dk Blue - ¾ ounce, (20 grams, 50 yards)
Crochet hook, size K (6.50 mm) **or** size needed
    for gauge
Yarn needle
½ yard 44/45" wide fabric
12" purchased pillow form **or** polyester fiberfill

Note: Entire Pillow is worked holding 2 strands of yarn
together.

GAUGE SWATCH: 4½" square
Work same as Square through Rnd 3.

SQUARE (Make 2)
Work same as Moroccan Tile Afghan Square A, page 72.

FINISHING
Using crocheted piece for pattern and adding ¼" seam
allowance, cut 2 pieces of fabric.
With **right** sides together, sew seam, leaving an opening for
turning.
Turn form right side out; insert pillow form **or** stuff firmly
with polyester fiberfill and sew opening closed.

JOINING
With Ecru and working through inside loops only,
whipstitch Squares together **(Fig. 26a, page 126)**,
inserting pillow form before closing.

For a Baby Boy (continued from page 76)

REMAINING 10 STRIPS
Work same as First Strip through Rnd 3 of Border: 404 sts.
Rnd 4 (Joining rnd): With **right** side facing, join White
with slip st in marked dc, remove marker; ch 1, sc in same
st, ★ skip next 2 sts, dc in next sc, (ch 1, dc in same st) 3
times, skip next 2 sts, (sc, ch 3, sc) in next dc; repeat from
★ once **more**, slip st in next hdc, [skip next st, (sc, ch 3,
sc) in next st, skip next st, slip st in next st] 47 times, [(sc,
ch 3, sc) in next dc, skip next 2 sts, dc in next sc, (ch 1, dc
in same st) 3 times, skip next 2 sts] twice, sc in next dc,
ch 1, holding Strips with **wrong** sides together and bottom
edges at the same end, sc in corresponding ch-3 sp on
previous Strip (Fig. 24, page 126), ch 1, sc in same st on
new Strip, slip st in next hdc, † skip next st, sc in next st,
ch 1, sc in next ch-3 sp on **previous Strip**, ch 1, sc in same
st on **new Strip**, skip next st, slip st in next st †, repeat
from † to † across, sc in same st as first sc, ch 1, sc in next
ch-3 sp on **previous Strip**, ch 1; join with slip st to first sc
on **new Strip**, finish off.

Grandparents Day (continued from page 78)

PLACEMENT DIAGRAM

B	B	B	B	B	B
B	A	A	A	A	B
B	A	A	A	A	B
B	A	A	A	A	B
B	A	A	A	A	B
B	A	A	A	A	B
B	A	A	A	A	B
B	B	B	B	B	B

EDGING
Rnd 1: With **right** side facing, join Black with sc in any
corner ch-3 sp **(see Joining With Sc, page 125)**; ch 2,
sc in same sp, ★ † ch 1, skip next dc, sc in next dc, ch 1,
(sc in next ch-1 sp, ch 1, skip next dc, sc in next dc, ch 1)
5 times, [(sc in next sp, ch 1) twice, skip next dc, sc in next
dc, ch 1, (sc in next ch-1 sp, ch 1, skip next dc, sc
in next dc, ch 1) 5 times] across to next corner ch-3 sp †,
(sc, ch 2, sc) in corner ch-3 sp; repeat from ★ 2 times **more**,
then repeat from † to † once; join with slip st to first sc, do
not finish off: 364 sps.

Instructions continued on page 116.

Rnds 2 and 3: Slip st in first corner ch-2 sp, ch 1, (sc, ch 2, sc) in same sp, ch 1, (sc in next ch-1 sp, ch 1) across to next corner ch-2 sp, ★ (sc, ch 2, sc) in corner ch-2 sp, ch 1, (sc in next ch-1 sp, ch 1) across to next corner ch-2 sp; repeat from ★ 2 times **more**; join with slip st to first sc: 372 sps.
Finish off.

Rnd 4: With **right** side facing, join Rose with slip st in any corner ch-2 sp; ch 3, (2 dc, ch 3, 3 dc) in same sp, ch 1, skip next ch-1 sp, (3 dc in next ch-1 sp, ch 1, skip next ch-1 sp) across to next corner ch-2 sp, ★ (3 dc, ch 3, 3 dc) in corner ch-2 sp, ch 1, skip next ch-1 sp, (3 dc in next ch-1 sp, ch 1, skip next ch-1 sp) across to next corner ch-2 sp; repeat from ★ 2 times **more**; join with slip st to first dc, finish off: 190 sps.

Rnd 5: With **right** side facing, join Lt Rose with slip st in any corner ch-3 sp; ch 3, (2 dc, ch 3, 3 dc) in same sp, ch 1, (3 dc in next ch-1 sp, ch 1) across to next corner ch-3 sp, ★ (3 dc, ch 3, 3 dc) in corner ch-3 sp, ch 1, (3 dc in next ch-1 sp, ch 1) across to next corner ch-3 sp; repeat from ★ 2 times **more**; join with slip st to first dc, finish off: 194 sps.

Rnd 6: With **right** side facing, join Black with slip st in any corner ch-3 sp; ch 3, (2 dc, ch 3, 3 dc) in same sp, ch 1, (3 dc in next ch-1 sp, ch 1) across to next corner ch-3 sp, ★ (3 dc, ch 3, 3 dc) in corner ch-3 sp, ch 1, (3 dc in next ch-1 sp, ch 1) across to next corner ch-3 sp; repeat from ★ 2 times **more**; join with slip st to first dc, finish off.

Rnd 7: With **right** side facing, join Green with slip st in any corner ch-3 sp; ch 3, (2 dc, ch 3, 3 dc) in same sp, ch 1, (3 dc in next ch-1 sp, ch 1) across to next corner ch-3 sp, ★ (3 dc, ch 3, 3 dc) in corner ch-3 sp, ch 1, (3 dc in next ch-1 sp, ch 1) across to next corner ch-3 sp; repeat from ★ 2 times **more**; join with slip st to first dc, finish off.

Rnd 8: With **right** side facing, join Lt Green with slip st in any corner ch-3 sp; ch 3, (2 dc, ch 3, 3 dc) in same sp, ch 1, (3 dc in next ch-1 sp, ch 1) across to next corner ch-3 sp, ★ (3 dc, ch 3, 3 dc) in corner ch-3 sp, ch 1, (3 dc in next ch-1 sp, ch 1) across to next corner ch-3 sp; repeat from ★ 2 times **more**; join with slip st to first dc, finish off.

Rnd 9: With **right** side facing, join Black with slip st in any corner ch-3 sp; ch 3, (2 dc, ch 3, 3 dc) in same sp, ch 1, (3 dc in next ch-1 sp, ch 1) across to next corner ch-3 sp, ★ (3 dc, ch 3, 3 dc) in corner ch-3 sp, ch 1, (3 dc in next ch-1 sp, ch 1) across to next corner ch-3 sp; repeat from ★ 2 times **more**; join with slip st to first dc, do **not** finish off.

Rnd 10: Slip st in next dc, ch 1, (slip st, ch 2, slip st) in next corner ch-3 sp, ch 1, ★ skip next dc, slip st in next dc, ch 1, (slip st in next ch-1 sp, ch 1, skip next dc, slip st in next dc, ch 1) across to next corner ch-3 sp, (slip st, ch 2, slip st) in corner ch-3 sp, ch 1; repeat from ★ 2 times **more**, skip next dc, (slip st in next dc, ch 1, slip st in next ch-1 sp, ch 1, skip next st) across; join with slip st to first slip st, finish off.

ASSEMBLY

Place two Panels together with bottom edges at the same end. Working through both loops, whipstitch Panels together (**Fig. 26b, page 126**), beginning in center dc of first corner and ending in center dc of next corner.

EDGING

Rnd 1: With **right** side facing, join yarn with slip st in center dc of top right corner; ch 4, (dc, ch 1, work V-St) in same st, skip next ch-1 sp, work V-St in each ch-1 sp across to within one ch-1 sp of center dc on next corner, skip ch-1 sp, ★ work (V-St, ch 1, V-St) in center dc, skip next ch-1 sp, work V-St in each ch-1 sp across to within one ch-1 sp of center dc on next corner, skip ch-1 sp; repeat from ★ around; join with slip st to first dc.

Rnd 2: Slip st in first ch-1 sp, ch 4, dc in same sp, work (V-St, ch 1, V-St) in next ch-1 sp, ★ work V-St in each ch-1 sp across to next corner ch-1 sp, work (V-St, ch 1, V-St) in corner ch-1 sp; repeat from ★ 2 times **more**, work V-St in each ch-1 sp across; join with slip st to first dc, finish off.

Note: Entire Pillow is worked holding 4 strands of yarn together.

GAUGE: 6 sc and 6 rows = 3"

Gauge Swatch: 3" square
Holding 4 stands of Red together, ch 7 **loosely**.
Row 1: Sc in second ch from hook and in each ch across: 6 sc.
Rows 2-6: Ch 1, turn; sc in each sc across.
Finish off.

STITCH GUIDE

DECREASE
Pull up a loop in next 2 sts, YO and draw through all 3 loops on hook (**counts as one sc**).

BODY

Holding 4 strands of Red together, ch 20 **loosely**.
Row 1 (Right side): 2 Sc in second ch from hook, decrease 3 times, sc in next 2 chs, 3 sc in next ch, sc in next 2 chs, decrease 3 times, 2 sc in last ch: 17 sc.
Note: Loop a short piece of yarn around any stitch to mark Row 1 as **right** side.

Row 2: Ch 1, turn; 2 sc in first sc, sc in next sc, pull up a loop in next 3 sts, YO and draw through all 4 loops on hook, sc in next 3 sc, 3 sc in next sc, sc in next 3 sc, pull up a loop in next 3 sts, YO and draw through all 4 loops on hook, sc in next sc, 2 sc in last sc: 17 sc.

Rows 3-5: Ch 1, turn; 2 sc in first sc, sc in each st across to last sc, 2 sc in last sc: 23 sc.

Rows 6-18: Ch 1, turn; sc in each sc across.

Rows 19 and 20: Ch 1, turn; decrease, sc in each sc across to last 2 sc, decrease: 19 sc.

RIGHT TOP

Row 1: Ch 1, turn; decrease, sc in next 5 sc, decrease, leave remaining 10 sc unworked: 7 sc.

Row 2: Ch 1, turn; decrease, sc in next 3 sc, decrease: 5 sc.

Row 3: Ch 1, turn; decrease, sc in next sc, decrease; finish off: 3 sc.

LEFT TOP

Row 1: With **right** side facing, skip first unworked sc on Row 20 of Body, join 4 strands of Red with slip st in next sc; ch 1, pull up a loop in same st and in next sc, YO and draw through all 3 loops on hook, sc in next 5 sc, decrease: 7 sc.

Row 2: Ch 1, turn; decrease, sc in next 3 sc, decrease: 5 sc.

Row 3: Ch 1, turn; decrease, sc in next sc, decrease; do **not** finish off: 3 sc.

EDGING

Ch 1, sc in end of each row across; working in free loops of beginning ch *(Fig. 21b, page 125)*, sc in first 3 chs, 2 sc in each of next 2 chs, sc in next 3 chs, pull up a loop in next 3 chs, YO and draw through all 4 loops on hook, sc in next 3 chs, 2 sc in each of next 2 chs, sc in next 3 chs; sc in end of each row across; 2 sc in first sc, sc in next sc, 2 sc in last sc; sc in end of first 3 rows; sc in skipped sc on Row 20 of Body; sc in end of next 3 rows; 2 sc in first sc, sc in next sc, 2 sc in last sc; join with slip st to first sc, finish off: 84 sc.

Repeat for second side; do **not** finish off.

JOINING

Holding **wrong** sides of Body together, matching stitches, and working through both loops of both pieces, slip st in each sc around, stuffing firmly with polyester fiberfill before closing; join with slip st to first slip st, finish off.

LEAF

Holding 4 strands of Green together, ch 11 **loosely**.

Row 1: 2 Dc in fourth ch from hook, tr in next 3 chs, dc in next ch, hdc in next ch, sc in next ch, 3 slip sts in last ch; working in free loops of beginning ch, sc in next ch, hdc in next ch, dc in next ch, tr in next 3 chs, 2 sc in next ch; join with slip st to top of beginning ch, finish off leaving a long end for sewing.

STEM

Holding 4 strands of Brown together, ch 11 **loosely**.

Row 1: Slip st in fourth ch from hook, dc in each ch across, finish off leaving a long end for sewing.

Using photo as a guide for placement, sew leaf and stem to Apple.

Warm Wishes (continued from page 84)

STITCH GUIDE

SC DECREASE
Pull up a loop in next 2 sts, YO and draw through all 3 loops on hook **(counts as one sc)**.

HDC DECREASE (uses next 2 sc)
★ YO, insert hook in **next** sc, YO and pull up a loop; repeat from ★ once **more**, YO and draw through all 5 loops on hook.

REVERSE SINGLE CROCHET
  (abbreviated reverse sc)
Working from **left** to **right**, insert hook in sc to right of hook, YO and draw through, under, and to left of loop on hook (2 loops on hook), YO and draw through both loops on hook *(Figs. 19a-d, page 125)*.

SOLE

Ch 7 **loosely**.

Row 1: Sc in second ch from hook and in each ch across: 6 sc.

Rows 2 and 3: Ch 1, turn; 2 sc in first sc, sc in each sc across to last sc, 2 sc in last sc: 10 sc.

Rows 4-18: Ch 1, turn; sc in each sc across.

Row 19: Ch 1, turn; 2 sc in first sc, sc in each sc across to last sc, 2 sc in last sc: 12 sc.

Row 20: Ch 1, turn; sc in each sc across.

Row 21: Ch 1, turn; 2 sc in first sc, sc in each sc across to last sc, 2 sc in last sc: 14 sc.

Rows 22-29: Ch 1, turn; sc in each sc across.

Rows 30-33: Ch 1, turn; pull up a loop in first 2 sts, YO and draw through all 3 loops on hook, sc in each sc across to last 2 sts, sc decrease; at end of Row 33, do **not** finish off: 6 sts.

Instructions continued on page 118.

Warm Wishes (continued from page 117)

EDGING

Rnd 1 (Right side)**:** Ch 1, turn; 2 sc in first sc, sc in next 4 sc, 2 sc in last st; sc in end of each row across; working in free loops of beginning ch *(Fig. 21b, page 125)*, sc in first 3 chs, place marker around last sc made to mark **right** side and Side placement, sc in next 3 chs; sc in end of each row across; join with slip st to Front Loop Only of first sc *(Fig. 20, page 125)*: 80 sc.

Rnd 2: Ch 1, turn; sc in Back Loop Only of same st and each sc around; join with slip st to **both** loops of first sc, finish off.

SIDES AND INSTEP

Rnd 1: With **right** side facing and working in free loops on Rnd 1 of Edging *(Fig. 21a, page 125)*, join yarn with sc in marked sc *(see Joining With Sc, page 125)*; sc in next sc and in each sc around; join with slip st to first sc.

Rnd 2: Ch 1, do **not** turn; sc in same st and in each sc around; join with slip st to first sc.

Rnd 3: Ch 2, hdc in next 34 sc, hdc decrease 5 times, hdc in each sc around; join with slip st to top of beginning ch-2: 75 sts.

Rnd 4: Ch 1, sc in same st and in next 34 hdc, sc decrease 3 times, sc in each hdc around; join with slip st to first sc, finish off: 72 sc.

Rnd 5: Ch 1, sc in same st and in next 33 sc, sc decrease 3 times, sc in each sc around; join with slip st to first sc: 69 sc.

Rnd 6: Ch 1, sc in same st and in next 30 sc, sc decrease 5 times, sc in each sc around; join with slip st to first sc: 64 sc.

Rnd 7: Ch 1, sc in same st and in next 30 sc, sc decrease 3 times, sc in each sc around; join with slip st to first sc: 61 sc.

Rnd 8: Ch 1, sc in same st and in next 29 sc, sc decrease 3 times, sc in each sc around; join with slip st to first sc: 58 sc.

Rnd 9: Ch 1, sc in same st and in next 22 sc, place marker around last sc made for seam placement, sc in next 6 sc, sc decrease 3 times, sc in next 7 sc, place marker around last sc made for seam placement, sc in each sc around; join with slip st to first sc, finish off: 55 sc.

With **right** sides together, sew Instep seam to marked sc.

CUFF

Rnd 1: With **right** side facing, join yarn with sc in same st as joining on Rnd 9; sc in next 20 sc, sc decrease, sc in each sc around; join with slip st to first sc, finish off: 37 sc.

Rnd 2: Ch 2, hdc in next sc and in each sc around; join with slip st to top of beginning ch-2.

Rnd 3: Ch 1, sc in same st and in each hdc around; join with slip st to first sc.

Rnd 4: Ch 1; working from **left** to **right**, work reverse sc in each sc around; join with slip st to first st, finish off.

Cut eight 8" lengths of yarn. Holding all strands together, tie around sc decrease on Rnd 1 of Cuff.

Roses Are Red (continued from page 86)

Rnd 7: Slip st in first ch-1 sp, ch 1, 2 sc in same sp, sc in each dc across to next corner ch-1 sp, ★ 3 sc in corner ch-1 sp, sc in each dc across to next corner ch-1 sp; repeat from ★ around, sc in same sp as first sc; join with slip st to first sc: 540 sc.

Rnds 8-13: Ch 1, 2 sc in same st, sc in each sc around working 3 sc in each corner sc, sc in same st as first sc; join with slip st to first sc: 588 sc.

Rnd 14: Ch 4, 2 dc in same st, dc in next sc and in each sc across to next corner sc, ★ (2 dc, ch 1, 2 dc) in corner sc, dc in next sc and in each sc across to next corner sc; repeat from ★ around, dc in same st as first dc; join with slip st to first dc: 600 dc.

Rnds 15 and 16: Repeat Rnd 5, twice; at end of Rnd 16, finish off: 632 dc.

Rnd 17: With **right** side facing, join Green with slip st in any corner ch-1 sp; ch 4, 2 dc in same sp, dc in each dc across to next corner ch-1 sp, ★ (2 dc, ch 1, 2 dc) in corner ch-1 sp, dc in each dc across to next corner ch-1 sp; repeat from ★ around, dc in same sp as first dc; join with slip st to first dc, finish off: 648 dc.

Rnd 18: With **right** side facing, join Ecru with slip st in any corner ch-1 sp; ch 4, 2 dc in same sp, dc in each dc across to next corner ch-1 sp, ★ (2 dc, ch 1, 2 dc) in corner ch-1 sp, dc in each dc across to next corner ch-1 sp; repeat from ★ around, dc in same sp as first dc; join with slip st to first dc: 664 dc.

Rnds 19-27: Repeat Rnd 5, 9 times; at end of Rnd 27, finish off: 808 dc.

Rnd 28: Repeat Rnd 17: 824 dc.

Rnd 29: With **right** side facing, join Ecru with slip st in any corner ch-1 sp; ch 1, (3 sc in corner ch-1 sp, sc in each dc across to next corner ch-1 sp) around; join with slip st to first sc: 836 sc.

Rnd 30: Ch 1, sc in same st, ch 3, sc in top of sc just worked *(Fig. 25, page 126)*, skip next sc, ★ sc in next sc, ch 3, sc in top of sc just worked, skip next sc; repeat from ★ around; join with slip st to first sc, finish off: 418 sc.

ROSE (Make 20)

With Red and small size hook, ch 4; join with slip st to form a ring.

Rnd 1 (Wrong side): Ch 1, (sc in ring, ch 3) 4 times; join with slip st to first sc: 4 ch-3 sps.

Rnd 2: Ch 1, (sc, 5 dc, sc) in each ch-3 sp around; join with slip st to first sc: 4 petals.

Rnd 3: Ch 1, working in **front** of petals, sc around post of first sc on Rnd 1 *(Fig. 10, page 123)*, ch 3, (sc around post of next sc on Rnd 1, ch 3) 3 times; join with slip st to first sc: 4 ch-3 sps.

Rnd 4: Ch 1, (sc, 5 tr, sc) in each ch-3 sp around; join with slip st to first sc: 4 petals.

Rnd 5: Ch 1, working in **front** of petals, sc around post of first sc on Rnd 3, ch 3, sc around post of next sc on Rnd 3, ch 3, sc in base of center tr on next petal, ch 3, (sc around post of next sc on Rnd 3, ch 3) twice, sc in base of center tr on next petal, ch 3; join with slip st to first sc: 6 ch-3 sps.

Rnd 6: Ch 1, (sc, 7 tr, sc) in each ch-3 sp around; join with slip st to first sc, finish off: 6 petals.

Sew edges of first petal together to form center bud.

ROSE LEAF (Make 20)

With Green and small size hook, ch 8 **loosely**.

Rnd 1 (Right side): Dc in fourth ch from hook, hdc in next 2 chs, sc in next ch, 3 sc in last ch; working in free loops of beginning ch, sc in next ch, hdc in next 2 chs, (dc, ch 3, slip st) in next ch; do **not** join.

Rnd 2: (Ch 1, slip st in next st) around; finish off leaving a long end for sewing.

VIOLET (Make 20)

With Purple and small size hook, ch 4; join with slip st to form a ring.

Rnd 1: (Ch 2, 3 dc, ch 2, slip st) 3 times in ring (bottom petals made), work (ch 3, 4 tr, ch 3, slip st) twice in ring (top petals made); finish off leaving a long end for sewing.

VIOLET LEAF (Make 20)

With Green and small size hook, ch 9 **loosely**.

Rnd 1: 4 Tr in fourth ch from hook, 2 tr in next ch, dc in next ch, hdc in next ch, sc in next ch, work 3 slip sts in last ch; working in free loops of beginning ch, sc in next ch, hdc in next ch, dc in next ch, 2 tr in next ch, work (4 tr, ch 3, slip st) in next ch; finish off leaving a long end for sewing.

FINISHING

With a single strand of Purple and following Charts, add cross-stitched words on Rnds 7-13 of Edging *(Fig. 29, page 127)*. Using double strands of Red, cross stitch hearts. Using photo as a guide for placement, sew Roses, Violets, and Leaves to Edging.

CHARTS

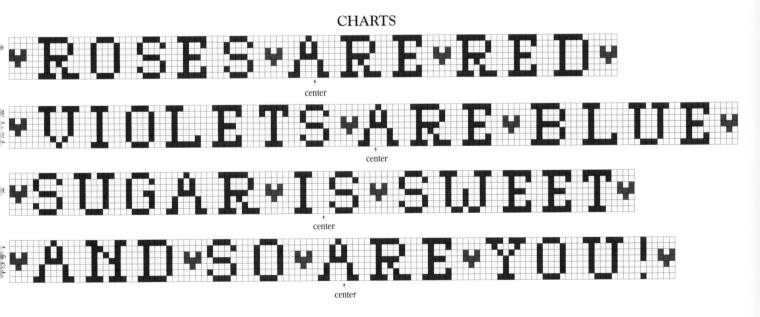

Easter Blossoms (continued from page 90)

Rnd 9: Ch 2, 3 hdc in next hdc, ★ hdc in next st and in each st across to center hdc of next corner 3-hdc group, 3 hdc in next hdc; repeat from ★ 2 times **more**, hdc in next st and in each st across; join with slip st to first hdc, finish off: 96 hdc.

ASSEMBLY

With Rose and working through both loops, whipstitch Squares together *(Fig. 26b, page 126)*, forming 5 vertical strips of 7 Squares each, beginning in center hdc of first corner and ending in center hdc of next corner; whipstitch strips together in same manner.

EDGING

Rnd 1: With **right** side facing, join Green with slip st in center hdc of any corner 3-hdc group; ch 2, 4 hdc in same st, ★ † hdc in next 24 hdc, 2 hdc in joining, (hdc in next 25 hdc, 2 hdc in joining) across to last Square, hdc in next 24 hdc †, 5 hdc in next hdc; repeat from ★ 2 times **more**, then repeat from † to † once; join with slip st to first hdc, finish off: 652 hdc.

Rnd 2: With **right** side facing, join Off-White with slip st in center hdc of any corner 5-hdc group; ch 1, 3 sc in same st, sc in next hdc and in each hdc across to center hdc of next corner 5-hdc group, ★ 3 sc in next hdc, sc in next hdc and in each hdc across to center hdc of next corner 5-hdc group; repeat from ★ around; join with slip st to first sc: 660 sc.

Rnd 3: Slip st in next sc, ch 1, sc in same st, ch 3, skip next 2 sc, ★ sc in next sc, ch 3, skip next 2 sc; repeat from ★ around; join with slip st to first sc: 220 ch-3 sps.

Rnd 4: Slip st in next ch-3 sp, ch 1, 4 sc in same sp, ★ 4 sc in each ch-3 sp across to next corner, ch 1; repeat from ★ around; join with slip st to first sc, finish off.

All-American (continued from page 92)

Row 4: Ch 3 **(counts as first dc, now and throughout)**, turn; work LDC in next 2 skipped sc 3 rows **below**, dc in next sc, ★ ch 2, skip next 2 sc, dc in next sc, work LDC in next 2 skipped sc 3 rows **below**, dc in next sc; repeat from ★ across: 104 dc and 25 ch-2 sps.

Row 5: Ch 1, turn; sc in first 4 dc, ★ ch 2, skip next ch-2 sp, sc in next 4 dc; repeat from ★ across changing to Ecru in last sc.

Row 6: Ch 5, turn; skip next 2 sc, dc in next sc, ★ work LDC in next 2 skipped sc 3 rows **below**, dc in next sc, ch 2, skip next 2 sc, dc in next sc; repeat from ★ across: 102 dc and 26 ch-2 sps.

Row 7: Ch 1, turn; sc in first dc, ch 2, skip next ch-2 sp, ★ sc in next 4 dc, ch 2, skip next ch-2 sp; repeat from ★ across to last dc, sc in last dc changing to Blue.

Row 8: Ch 3, turn; work LDC in next 2 skipped sc 3 rows **below**, dc in next sc, ★ ch 2, skip next 2 sc, dc in next sc, work LDC in next 2 skipped sc 3 rows **below**, dc in next sc; repeat from ★ across: 104 dc and 25 ch-2 sps.

Row 9: Ch 1, turn; sc in first 4 dc, ★ ch 2, skip next ch-2 sp, sc in next 4 dc; repeat from ★ across changing to Dk Blue in last sc.

Row 10: Ch 5, turn; skip next 2 sc, dc in next sc, ★ work LDC in next 2 skipped sc 3 rows **below**, dc in next sc, ch 2, skip next 2 sc, dc in next sc; repeat from ★ across: 102 dc and 26 ch-2 sps.

Row 11: Ch 1, turn; sc in first dc, ch 2, skip next ch-2 sp, ★ sc in next 4 dc, ch 2, skip next ch-2 sp; repeat from ★ across to last dc, sc in last dc changing to Burgundy.

Rows 12-183: Repeat Rows 4-11, 21 times; then repeat Rows 4-7 once **more**.

Row 184: Ch 1, turn; sc in first sc, work LSC in next 2 skipped sc 3 rows **below**, ★ sc in next 4 sc, work LSC in next 2 skipped sc 3 rows **below**; repeat from ★ across to last sc, sc in last sc; do **not** finish off.

EDGING

Rnd 1: Ch 1, do **not** turn; 2 sc in last sc made on Row 184, sc evenly spaced across end of rows; working in free loops of beginning ch *(Fig. 21b, page 125)*, 3 sc in ch at base of first sc, sc in each ch across to last ch, 3 sc in last ch; sc evenly spaced across end of rows; working across sts on Row 184, 3 sc in first sc, sc in each sc across, sc in same st as first sc; join with slip st to first sc.

Rnd 2: Ch 1, 2 sc in same st, sc in each sc around working 3 sc in each corner 3-sc group, sc in same st as first sc; join with slip st to first sc.

Rnd 3: Ch 1, work reverse sc in each sc around; join with slip st to first st, finish off.

A Family Noel (continued from page 98)

PLACEMENT DIAGRAM

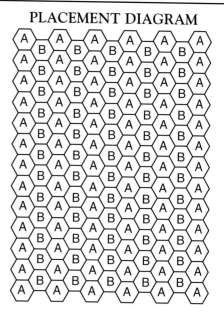

GENERAL INSTRUCTIONS

BASIC INFORMATION

ABBREVIATIONS

BPdc	Back Post double crochet(s)
BPsc	Back Post single crochet(s)
BPtr	Back Post treble crochet(s)
ch(s)	chain(s)
dc	double crochet(s)
Dk	Dark
dtr	double treble crochet(s)
FPdc	Front Post double crochet(s)
FPtr	Front Post treble crochet(s)
hdc	half double crochet(s)
LFPtr	Long Front Post treble crochet(s)
Lt	Light
mm	millimeters
Med	Medium
Rnd(s)	Round(s)
sc	single crochet(s)
sp(s)	space(s)
st(s)	stitch(es)
tr	treble crochet(s)
tr tr	triple treble crochet(s)
YO	yarn over

SYMBOLS

★ — work instructions following ★ as many **more** times as indicated in addition to the first time.

† to † — work all instructions from first † to second † as **many** times as specified.

( ) or [ ] — work enclosed instructions **as many** times as specified by the number immediately following **or** work all enclosed instructions in the stitch or space indicated **or** contains explanatory remarks.

colon (:) — the number(s) given after a colon at the end of a row or round denote(s) the number of stitches you should have on that row or round.

TERMS

chain loosely — work the chain **only** loose enough for the hook to pass through the chain easily when working the next row or round into the chain.

multiple — the number of stitches required to complete one repeat of a pattern.

post — the vertical shaft of a stitch.

right side vs. wrong side — the **right** side of your work is the side that will show when the piece is finished.

work across or around — continue working in the established pattern.

GAUGE

Gauge is the number of stitches and rows or rounds per inch and is used to determine the finished size of a project. All crochet patterns will specify the gauge that you must match to ensure proper size and to ensure that you have enough yarn to complete the project.

Hook size given in instructions is merely a guide. Because everyone crochets differently — loosely, tightly, or somewhere in between — the finished size can vary, even when crocheters use the very same pattern, yarn, and hook. Before beginning any crocheted item, it is absolutely necessary for you to crochet a gauge swatch in the pattern stitch indicated and using the weight of yarn and hook size suggested. Your swatch must be large enough to measure your gauge. Lay your swatch on a hard, smooth, flat surface. Then measure it, counting your stitches and rows or rounds carefully. If your swatch is smaller than specified or you have too many stitches per inch, try again with a larger size hook; if your swatch is larger than specified or you don't have enough stitches per inch, try again with a smaller size hook. Keep trying until you find the size that will give you the specified gauge. DO NOT HESITATE TO CHANGE HOOK SIZE TO OBTAIN CORRECT GAUGE. Once proper gauge is obtained, measure width of piece approximately every 3" to be sure gauge remains consistent.

BASIC STITCH GUIDE

CHAIN (*abbreviated ch*)

To work a chain stitch, begin with a slip knot on the hook. Bring the yarn **over** hook from **back** to **front**, catching the yarn with the hook and turning the hook slightly toward you to keep the yarn from slipping off. Draw the yarn through the slip knot (*Fig. 1*).

Fig. 1

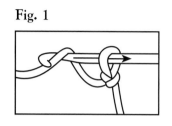

WORKING INTO THE CHAIN

When beginning a row of crochet in a chain, always skip the first chain from the hook and work into the second chain from hook (for single crochet), third chain from hook (for half double crochet), or fourth chain from hook (for double crochet), etc. (*Fig. 2a*).

Fig. 2a

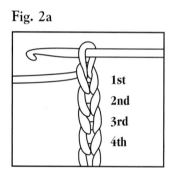

1st
2nd
3rd
4th

Method 1: Insert hook into back ridge of each chain indicated (*Fig. 2b*).
Method 2: Insert hook under top loop **and** the back ridge of each chain indicated (*Fig. 2c*).

Fig. 2b

Fig. 2c

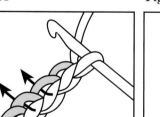
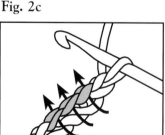

SLIP STITCH (*abbreviated slip st*)

This stitch is used to attach new yarn, to join work, or to move the yarn across a group of stitches without adding height. Insert hook in stitch or space indicated, YO and draw through stitch **and** loop on hook (*Fig. 3*).

Fig. 3

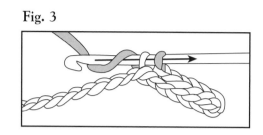

SINGLE CROCHET (*abbreviated sc*)

Insert hook in stitch or space indicated, YO and pull up a loop (2 loops on hook), YO and draw through both loops on hook (*Fig. 4*).

Fig. 4

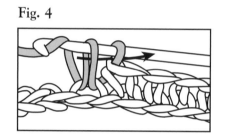

HALF DOUBLE CROCHET
(*abbreviated hdc*)

YO, insert hook in stitch or space indicated, YO and pull up a loop (3 loops on hook), YO and draw through all 3 loops on hook (*Fig. 5*).

Fig. 5

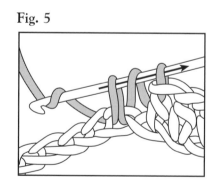

DOUBLE CROCHET
(abbreviated dc)
YO, insert hook in stitch or space indicated, YO and pull up a loop (3 loops on hook), YO and draw through 2 loops on hook (*Fig. 6a*), YO and draw through remaining 2 loops on hook (*Fig. 6b*).

Fig. 6a

Fig. 6b

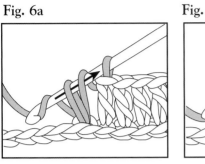

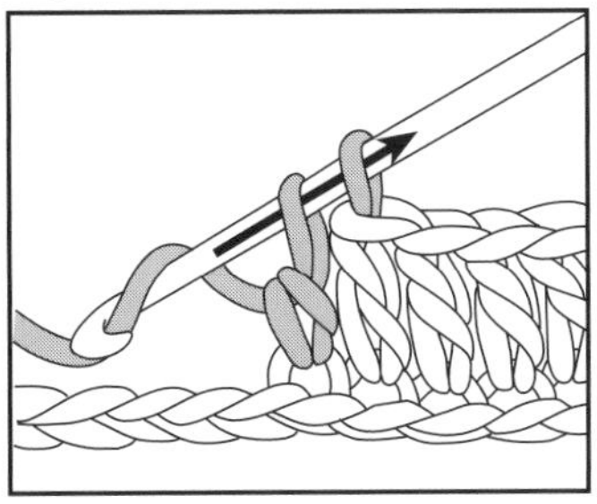

TREBLE CROCHET
(abbreviated tr)
YO twice, insert hook in stitch or space indicated, YO and pull up a loop (4 loops on hook) (*Fig. 7a*), (YO and draw through 2 loops on hook) 3 times (*Fig. 7b*).

Fig. 7a

Fig. 7b

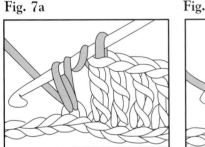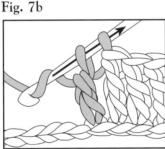

DOUBLE TREBLE CROCHET
(abbreviated dtr)
YO 3 times, insert hook in stitch or space indicated, YO and pull up a loop (5 loops on hook) (*Fig. 8a*), (YO and draw through 2 loops on hook) 4 times (*Fig. 8b*).

Fig. 8a

Fig. 8b

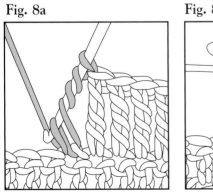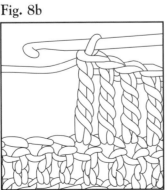

TRIPLE TREBLE CROCHET
(abbreviated tr tr)
YO 4 times, insert hook in stitch or space indicated, YO and pull up a loop (6 loops on hook) (*Fig. 9a*), (YO and draw through 2 loops on hook) 5 times (*Fig. 9b*).

Fig. 9a

Fig. 9b

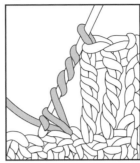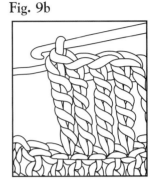

PATTERN STITCHES
POST STITCH
Work around post of stitch indicated, inserting hook in direction of arrow (*Fig. 10*).

Fig. 10

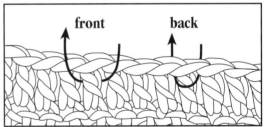

FRONT POST DOUBLE CROCHET (abbreviated FPdc)
YO, insert hook from **front** to **back** around post of stitch indicated (*Fig. 10*), YO and pull up a loop (3 loops on hook) (*Fig. 11*), (YO and draw through 2 loops on hook) twice.

Fig. 11

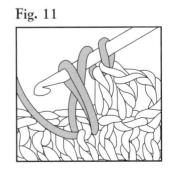

123

FRONT POST TREBLE CROCHET (abbreviated FPtr)

YO twice, insert hook from **front** to **back** around post of stitch indicated (*Fig. 10*), YO and pull up a loop (4 loops on hook) (*Fig. 12*), (YO and draw through 2 loops on hook) 3 times.

Fig. 12

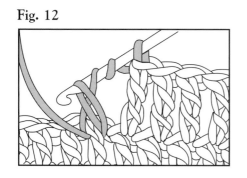

BACK POST SINGLE CROCHET (abbreviated BPsc)

Insert hook from **back** to **front** around post of stitch indicated (*Fig. 10*), YO and pull up a loop (*Fig. 13*), YO and draw through both loops on hook.

Fig. 13

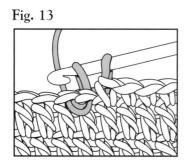

BACK POST DOUBLE CROCHET (abbreviated BPdc)

YO, insert hook from **back** to **front** around post of stitch indicated (*Fig. 10*), YO and pull up a loop (3 loops on hook) (*Fig. 14*), (YO and draw through 2 loops on hook) twice.

Fig. 14

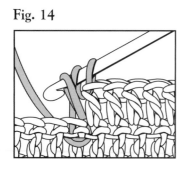

BACK POST TREBLE CROCHET (abbreviated BPtr)

YO twice, insert hook from **back** to **front** around post of stitch indicated (*Fig. 10*), YO and pull up a loop (4 loops on hook) (*Fig. 15*), (YO and draw through 2 loops on hook) 3 times.

Fig. 15

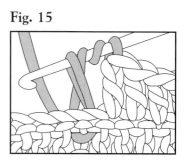

CLUSTER

A Cluster can be worked all in the same stitch or space (*Figs. 16a & b*), **or** across several stitches (*Figs. 17a & b*).

Fig. 16a

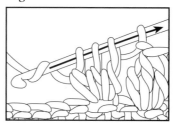

Fig. 16b

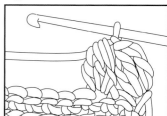

Fig. 17a

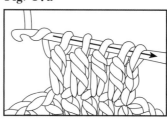

Fig. 17b

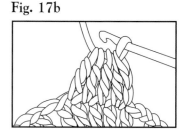

POPCORN

Work 4 dc in stitch or space indicated, drop loop from hook, insert hook in first st of 4-dc group, hook dropped loop and draw through (*Fig. 18*).

Fig. 18

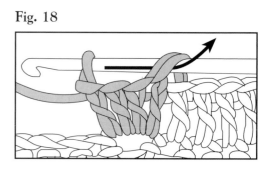

REVERSE SINGLE CROCHET
(abbreviated reverse sc)

Working from **left** to **right**, ★ insert hook in st to right of hook **(Fig. 19a)**, YO and draw through, under, and to left of loop on hook (2 loops on hook) **(Fig. 19b)**, YO and draw through both loops on hook **(Fig. 19c) (reverse sc made, Fig. 19d)**.

Fig. 19a

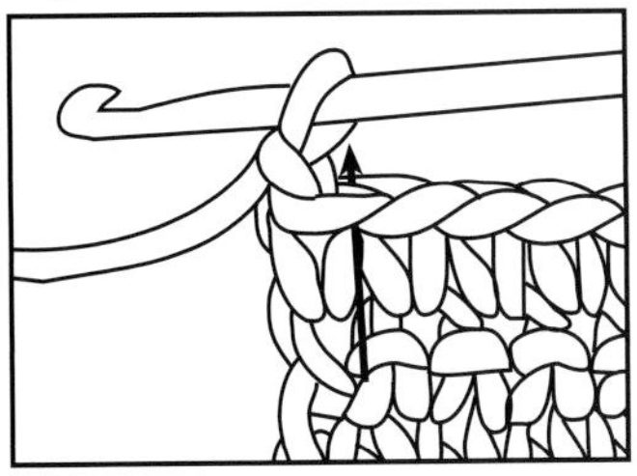

Fig. 19b

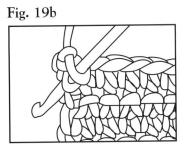

Fig. 19c

Fig. 19d

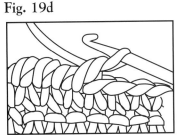

STITCHING TIPS

JOINING WITH SC

When instructed to join with sc, begin with a slip knot on hook. Insert hook in stitch or space indicated, YO and pull up a loop, YO and draw through both loops on hook.

BACK OR FRONT LOOP ONLY

Work only in loop(s) indicated by arrow **(Fig. 20)**.

Fig. 20

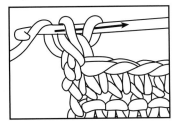

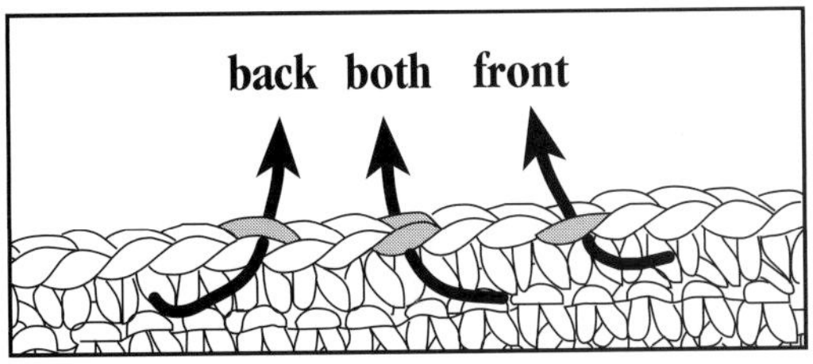

back   both   front

FREE LOOPS

After working in Back or Front Loops Only on a row or round, there will be a ridge of unused loops. These are called the free loops. Later, when instructed to work in the free loops of the same row or round, work in these loops **(Fig. 21a)**.

When instructed to work in a free loop of a beginning chain, work in loop indicated by arrow **(Fig. 21b)**.

Fig. 21a

Fig. 21b

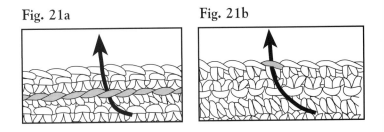

CHANGING COLORS

Work the last stitch to within one step of completion, hook new yarn **(Fig. 22a)** and draw through loops on hook. Cut old yarn and work over both ends unless otherwise specified. When working in rounds or changing colors with a slip stitch, cut old yarn; using new yarn, join with slip stitch to first stitch **(Fig. 22b)**.

Fig. 22a

Fig. 22b

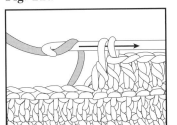
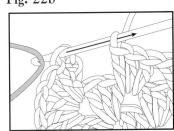

WORKING IN SPACE BEFORE STITCH

When instructed to work in space **before** a stitch or in spaces **between** stitches, insert hook in space indicated by arrow **(Fig. 23)**.

Fig. 23

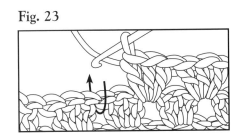

NO-SEW JOINING

Hold Squares, Motifs, or Strips with **wrong** sides together. Slip st or sc into sp as indicated **(Fig. 24)**.

Fig. 24

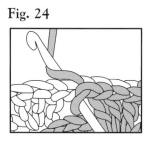

WORKING IN TOP OF STITCH

When instructed to work in top of stitch just worked, insert hook as indicated by arrow **(Fig. 25)**.

Fig. 25

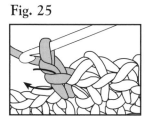

FINISHING

WHIPSTITCH

With **wrong** sides together and beginning in stitch indicated, sew through both pieces once to secure the beginning of the seam, leaving an ample yarn end to weave in later. Insert the needle from **front** to **back** through **inside** loops of each piece **(Fig. 26a)** or through **both** loops **(Fig. 26b)**. Bring the needle around and insert it from **front** to **back** through the next loops of **both** pieces. Continue in this manner across to stitch indicated, keeping the sewing yarn fairly loose and being careful to match stitches.

Fig. 26a

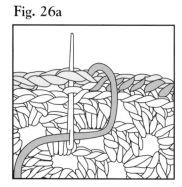

Fig. 26b

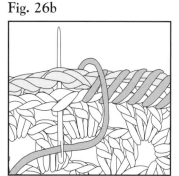

WASHING AND BLOCKING

Before washing or blocking your afghan, check the yarn label for any special instructions. Many acrylics and some blends have special handling instructions and may be damaged during washing and/or blocking.

Many fibers require hand washing. Carefully launder your afghan using a mild soap or detergent; rinse it without wringing or twisting. Remove any excess moisture by rolling it in a succession of dry towels. If you prefer, you may put it in the final spin cycle of your washer — but do **not** use water. Lay the afghan on a flat surface covered with towels out of direct sunlight. Gently smooth and pat afghan to the finished size as indicated in the individual instructions. Pin in place using stainless steel pins; when the afghan is completely dry, it is blocked.

Steaming is an excellent method of blocking afghans, especially those made with wool or wool blends. Turn the afghan to the **wrong** side. Using stainless steel pins, pin afghan on a board covered with towels to the finished size as indicated in the individual instructions. Hold a steam iron or steamer just above the afghan and steam it thoroughly. Never let the weight of the iron touch your item because it will flatten the stitches. Leave the afghan pinned until it is completely dry.

FRINGE

Cut a piece of cardboard 8" wide and 1/2" longer than desired fringe. Wind the yarn **loosely** and **evenly** around the length of the cardboard until the card is filled, then cut across one end; repeat as needed.

Align the number of strands desired and fold in half. With **wrong** side facing and using a crochet hook, draw the folded end up through a stitch, row, or loop, and pull the loose ends through the folded end **(Fig. 27a)**; draw the knot up **tightly** **(Fig. 27b)**. Repeat, spacing as desired. Lay flat on a hard surface and trim the ends.

Fig. 27a

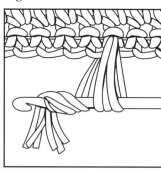

Fig. 27b

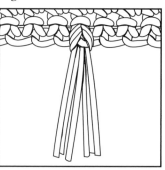

TASSEL

Cut a piece of cardboard 3" wide and 6" long. Wind a double strand of yarn around the cardboard approximately 12 times. Cut an 18" length of yarn and insert it under all strands at the top of the cardboard; pull up **tightly** and tie securely. Leave the yarn ends long enough to attach the tassel. Cut the yarn at the opposite end of the cardboard and then remove it *(Fig. 28a)*. Cut a 6" length of yarn and wrap it **tightly** around the tassel twice, 1" below the top *(Fig. 28b)*; tie securely. Trim ends.

Fig. 28a   **Fig. 28b**

EMBROIDERY STITCHES

CROSS STITCH

Each square on the Chart represents one sc and each shaded square represents one cross stitch. Thread a yarn needle with a long strand of color indicated. With **right** side facing and bottom edge toward you, bring needle up at 1, leaving a 3" end on back. Work over this end to secure. Insert needle down at 2 (half Cross made), bring needle up at 3 and go down at 4 (**Cross Stitch completed, *Fig. 29***). You can work across an area in half crosses and then work back, crossing them as you go. Just be sure that the top half of every cross stitch is worked in the same direction. After each row is worked, weave yarn through stitches on back to point where next cross is worked (long strands of yarn should not show on back). Straighten yarn every few crosses by dropping the needle and allowing the yarn to hang free, untwisting itself. Finish off by weaving under several stitches on back; cut yarn.

Fig. 29

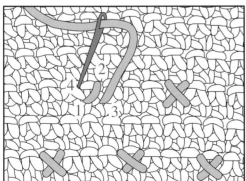

STRAIGHT STITCH

Straight Stitch is just what the name implies, a single, straight stitch. Bring needle up at 1 and go down at 2 *(Fig. 30)*. Continue in same manner.

Fig. 30

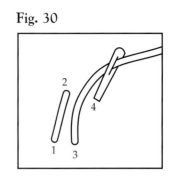

SATIN STITCH

Satin Stitch is a series of straight stitches entering and exiting the same hole *(Fig. 31)*. Bring needle up at odd numbers and go down at even numbers.

Fig. 31

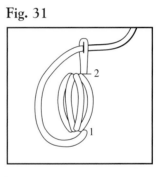

FRENCH KNOT

Bring needle up at 1. Wrap yarn desired number of times around needle and go down at 2, holding end of yarn with non-stitching fingers *(Fig. 32)*. Tighten knot; then pull needle through, holding yarn until it must be released.

Fig. 32

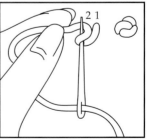

CREDITS

A special *thank you* to **Vanna White** of television's *Wheel of Fortune*
for welcoming our photography staff into her home.

We also wish to thank the generous people who allowed us to photograph
afghans at their homes: **James and Joan Adams** and **Michael and Karen Sage**.

To **Magna IV Color Imaging** of Little Rock, Arkansas, we say *thank you*
for the superb color reproduction and excellent pre-press preparation.

We want to especially thank our on-location photography stylist **Christina Myers** and photographer
Ralph Anderson for their time, patience, and excellent work. We also extend our thanks to
studio photographers **Ken West, Larry Pennington, Mark Mathews,** and **Karen Shirey** of Peerless
Photography, Little Rock, Arkansas, and **Jerry R. Davis** of Jerry Davis Photography, Little Rock, Arkansas.

We offer a special word of appreciation to the talented designers
who created the lovely projects in this book:

Eleanor Albano: *Rose Glow*, page 74

Alexander-Stratton: *Interlaced Links*, page 4, and *Pretty Pansies*, page 36

Mary Lamb Becker: *Mountain Trails*, page 16

Nancy Fuller: *Reversible Plaid*, page 107, and *Moroccan Tile*, page 72

Sarah J. Green: *Christmas Snowflakes*, page 98

Anne Halliday: *Kitty Cat Clusters*, page 14; *Magnolia*, page 18; *Tender Embrace*, page 54; *Cuddly Ripple*, page 56;
Elegant Clusters, page 68; *Heart Silhouettes*, page 70; *Victorian Granny*, page 78; and *Stylish Stripes*, page 84

Sheila Hardy: *Violets in Bloom*, page 28

Jan Hatfield: *Track and Field*, page 32

Carol L. Jensen: *Cozy Mittens*, page 38

Terry Kimbrough: *Loving Hearts*, page 6; *Teddy Bear*, page 58;
Apple Pillow, page 82; and *Romantic Cover-up*, page 86

Ann Kirtley: *Sweet Dreams*, page 40, and *Graceful Fans*, page 66

Jennine Korejko: *Lacy Mile-A-Minute*, page 22, and *Little Boy Blue*, page 76

Patricia Kristoffersen: *Soft Mile-A-Minute*, page 60

Cynthia Lark: *Granny's Dogwood*, page 90

Melissa Leapman: *Classic Argyle*, page 42; *Country Checks*, page 82; and *Patriotic Colors*, page 92

Carole Prior: *Birthstone Wrap*, page 12; *Waterfall Ripple*, page 34; *Sunny Sunflowers*, page 44;
Emerald Isle, page 88; and *Festive Stripes*, page 94

Katherine Satterfield: *Racing Stripes*, page 50, and *Baby Yo-Yo Pillowghan*, page 64

Ruth Shepherd: *Women's Booties*, page 84

Mary Ann Sipes: *Attic Windows*, page 20; *Double Wedding Ring*, page 52; and *Plush Comfort*, page 80

Martha Brooks Stein: *Bear's Paw*, page 30

Gail Tanquary: *Welcome Pineapples*, page 8, and *Cherub Filet*, page 48

Beth Ann Webber: *Angel Doll*, page 24; *Angelic Blossoms*, page 27; and *Enchanting Elf*, page 94

Maggie Weldon: *Bed of Roses*, page 10, and *Rich Diamonds*, page 62